1120 | | | Anglic
1, t

LOVE LETTERS

Grange + that I am
will flourish then
off the hand more
. Everything is

yrs Eternally — I adore you

LOVE LETTERS

INTIMATE CORRESPONDENCE BETWEEN FAMOUS LOVERS

Edited by Andrea Clarke

BRITISH LIBRARY

In loving memory of my father, David Clarke (1946–2011) 🐛

The author would like to thank the following for their invaluable assistance:
Jamie Andrews, Claire Breay, Helen Broderick, Eleanor Dickens, Julian
Harrison, Arnold Hunt, Kathryn Johnson, Scot McKendrick, Jill Purslow,
Lara Speicher, Michael St John-McAllister, Laura Walker and Zoe Wilcox.

(**Frontispiece**) Detail of letter from Mervyn Peake to his wife, Maeve
Gilmore, 17 August 1950.

CONTENTS

Introduction
PAGE 8

Isaias to her husband, Hephaestion, 29 August 168 BC
PAGE 14

Margery Brews to John Paston III, February 1477
PAGE 18

Prince Arthur to Katherine of Aragon, 5 October 1499
PAGE 22

Pierre Sala, *Petit Livre d'Amour* to Marguerite Bullioud, *c*.1500
PAGE 26

Anne Boleyn and Henry VIII, love notes, *c*.1528
PAGE 30

Katherine Parr to Henry VIII, July 1544
PAGE 34

Earl of Essex to Elizabeth I, 18 October 1591
PAGE 38

Sir Thomas Baskerville to his wife, Mary, 21 August 1595
PAGE 44

Thomas Knyvett to his wife, Katherine, 26 November 1621
PAGE 48

George Villiers to James I, 29 August 1623

PAGE 52

Dorothy Osborne to Sir William Temple, 15/16 October 1653

PAGE 58

Sir John Fenwick to his wife, Mary, January 1697

PAGE 62

Vanessa [Esther van Homrigh] to Jonathan Swift, 1714

PAGE 68

Horatio Nelson's last letter to Lady Emma Hamilton,
19 October 1805

PAGE 72

Charles Dickens to Catherine Hogarth, May 1835

PAGE 76

Charlotte Brontë to Professor Constantin Héger,
18 November 1845

PAGE 82

Elizabeth Barrett Browning, Sonnet 43 from
*Sonnets from the Portuguese, c.*1846

PAGE 86

George Elliot to Herbert Spencer, July 1852

PAGE 90

Dante Gabriel Rossetti to Jane Morris, 4 February 1870

PAGE 94

Christina Rossetti, Valentine poem to her mother, 1884
PAGE 98

Oscar Wilde to Lord Alfred Douglas, January 1897
PAGE 100

Gordon Bottomley to Emily Burton, 17 October 1899
PAGE 106

Rupert Brooke to Cathleen Nesbitt, 1913
PAGE 112

Roger Keyes to his wife, Eva, 10 December 1914
PAGE 118

Dora Carrington to Lytton Strachey, 7 June 1918
PAGE 122

Mervyn Peake to his wife, Maeve Gilmore, early 1940s
PAGE 126

Gerry Raffles to Joan Littlewood, 1 November 1948
PAGE 130

Ralph Richardson to his wife, Meriel Forbes, 1964–70
PAGE 134

Ted Hughes to Sylvia Plath, *c*.1980
PAGE 138

Picture Credits
PAGE 142

INTRODUCTION

In an age of emails, tweets and texted 'I luv u's', *Love Letters* invites us into a privileged realm and reminds us why the written word is so special. Drawn from the breadth and depth of the British Library's vast national collection of manuscripts, these handwritten, intimate exchanges between couples – some famous, others now lost to history – span centuries, cultures and continents.

Love letters are, by their very nature, private communications and some of those selected remained a secret between sender and recipient for years, not to be seen, as Margery Brews beseeches John Paston in 1477, 'by any earthly creature save only yourself'. Physically, love letters are, like many other manuscript letters, pieces of paper on which there is some writing. However, what makes them compelling to read and imbues them with a magical quality is the emotional bond between the sender and recipient, and, concomitantly, their perceived ability to transform life, transcend time and bridge distances. As Prince Arthur explains to Katherine of Aragon: 'Truly, your letters, traced by your own hand, have so delighted me, and have rendered me so cheerful and jocund, that I fancied I beheld your Highness and conversed with and embraced my dearest wife.' Similarly, Dante Gabriel Rossetti tells Jane Morris that 'it is so seldom that the dead hours breathe a little and yield your dear voice to me again. I seem to hear it while I write, and to see your eyes speaking as clearly as your voice.'

Love letters are an expression of intimacy; their words allow us insight into the private relationships of people down the ages. The exchanges selected here contain expressions of recognisable human emotions and every shade of love, from the joy of falling in love to the pain of unrequited love. Three amorous declarations from across the centuries are included: from the fifteenth century, the young Margery Brews's letter to John Paston, her 'right well-beloved Valentine', declares 'my heart bids me ever more to love you, truly over all earthly thing'; and Pierre Sala's exquisitely illuminated *Petit Livre d'Amour*, which he presented to Marguerite Bullioud, 'who since my childhood I have always wanted to love, serve, esteem and honour'. Gordon Bottomley's declaration of love, sent to Emily Burton in 1899 after five years of friendship, is particularly moving as he declares: 'O, how I hope that I am not estranging you even when I tell you that I love you wholly, that as long as I have known you, you have been to me "half angel and half bird and all a wonder and a wild desire", that your influence alone can waken what is best in me.'

Letters written during courtships also number among the present selection. Dorothy Osborne's charming letter, written in 1653 to her future husband, Sir William Temple, lists the 'great many ingredients that must go to making me happy in a husband'. In contrast, Charles Dickens's letter to his future wife, Catherine Hogarth, written, 'with the greatest pain', just three weeks into their engagement, reveals that he already harboured doubts about their suitability as marriage partners. Amorous exchanges written during passionate affairs also feature. Two love-notes entered in Anne Boleyn's Book of Hours by her and Henry VIII provide some of the earliest evidence for their love affair. The raw passion of love is perhaps best represented in the letter sent by Rupert Brooke to Cathleen Nesbitt, which he ends with the words 'I'm madly eager to see you again. My heart goes knocking when I think of it [...] I will kiss you till I kill you.'

Several of the selected letters are the deeply affectionate outpourings of tender and happy marriages: Norfolk landowner Thomas Knyvett's delightful letter, sent to his adored wife, Katherine, while away on business in London, to inform her that 'I have been to look for stuff for your bed, and have sent down patterns for you to choose which you like best'; Elizabeth Barrett Browning's sonnet, written for her devoted husband, Robert Browning, in which she asks 'How do I love thee? Let me count the ways'; and more recently, Mervyn Peake's wonderfully illustrated letter to his wife, Maeve, written shortly before she was due to give birth, in which he simply declares 'Maevie. I am in love. Deeply. Un-endingly, for ever and ever.'

Absence is the subject of several letters, beginning with one written on papyrus in 168 BC by Isaias to her husband, Hephaestion, a soldier in the Egyptian army who has failed to return home to his family. The tone of her letter ranges from loving irritation to incredulity to despair before she ends the letter by entreating him to return home. Katherine Parr, writing as Queen Regent in 1547 while Henry VIII was on a military campaign in France, reminds him that 'whereas I know your Majesty's absence is never without great respects of things most convenient and necessary, yet love and affection compelleth me to desire your presence'. Four hundred years later, Gerry Raffles likens himself to 'a camel who looks forward to the oasis 7 days ahead' as he eagerly awaits the return of Joan Littlewood.

There is often as much pain and grief in a love affair as pleasure, so it is appropriate that not all the letters in this book point to such happy endings as some of those already mentioned. Among the most heartrending items in this collection are those that deal with the final separation of loved ones. Tragedy and romance mingle in Sir John

Fenwick's letter to his wife, Mary, written in 1697, while awaiting execution for treason. Desperate to see her once more, he implores, 'Get to me, if possible, before I die … All my fear is I shall never see you.' Equally moving is devoted husband and distinguished naval officer Sir Roger Keyes's letter to his wife, Eva, written shortly before he embarked on the dangerous Cuxhaven Raid in December 1914, to ensure that in the event of his death she would know 'how blissfully happy I have been with you my Sweet Red Rose'.

Unrequited love is the theme of other letters in the collection, including Charlotte Brontë's desperate letter to Professor Constantin Héger, in which she confesses that 'truly I find it difficult to be cheerful so long as I think I shall never see you more'. The breath-stopping pain felt by Vanessa in her letter to Jonathan Swift and her sense of separation is real and devastating, as she writes, ''Tis impossible to describe what I have suffered since I saw you last; I am sure I could have bore the rack much better than those killing, killing words of yours. Sometimes I have resolved to die without seeing you more; but those resolves, to your misfortune, did not last long.' And, following Herbert Spencer's rejection of her, George Eliot implores, 'If you become attached to someone else, then I must die, but until then I could gather courage to work and make life valuable, if only I had you near me.'

The last category of letter included in this selection is the philosophical kind, written by those who reflect back on the end of a love affair. This is perhaps best represented by Oscar Wilde's exquisitely eloquent 50,000-word letter, written from Reading Gaol to his lover 'Bosie', which ends: 'You came to me to learn the pleasures of life and the pleasure of art. Perhaps I am chosen to teach you something much more wonderful. The meaning of sorrow, and its beauty, Your affectionate friend, Oscar Wilde.' Here also belongs the Poet Laureate Ted Hughes's verse-letter, entitled 'Cambridge was our courtship', in which he reflects on his early relationship with the poet Sylvia Plath.

The transcripts of the love letters selected here are all fascinating in their different ways, and paint a vivid picture of each couple – such is the power of words. But, as the accompanying images of the original manuscripts demonstrate, the letters are more than mere collections of words. Having flowed from the hands of the once-living, the letters also have a physical dimension and a palpable story to tell, summed up by Philip Larkin as the 'magical quality of manuscripts'. The physical appearance of the letters can often add another dimension to our understanding, from the revelation of character through handwriting to the actual physical constitution of a letter. Only an image of Margery Brews's letter to John Paston, for example, will reveal upon close inspection that she has made her initials, added to the end of the letter, look like a heart. Similarly, it is only when one sees an image of the original manuscript of Oscar Wilde's 'De Profundis' that one realises it is tear-stained, or that Charlotte Brontë's letters were torn to pieces and then sewn together again, or that Anne Boleyn and Henry VIII deliberately entered their messages to each other beneath highly significant illuminations in Anne's Book of Hours. It is far more poignant to see Emma Hamilton's handwritten, anguished note – 'Oh miserable wretched Emma, oh glorious & happy Nelson' – on his final, unfinished letter to her than it is to read it in a transcript. Looking at an image of the manuscript of the Earl of Essex's impassioned, noble letter to Elizabeth I, with its fold-lines still visible, one starts to imagine the Queen loosening its silk ties, breaking the wax seal, and unfolding the letter...

The present selection of love letters are all survivals from the past, and their survival also tells a story; some of them we know, others we are left to imagine. While we can only speculate, for example, that Hephaestion returned to Isaias in such haste after receiving her letter that he left the papyrus behind in the temple, where it was discovered centuries later, we *do* know that Robert Browning treasured the tiny notebook containing Elizabeth Barrett Browning's *Sonnets from the Portuguese* long after her death. Similarly, following the loss of his beloved wife, Emily, Gordon Bottomley treasured their correspondence, sealing each letter in envelopes that would remain unopened for decades, before their purchase by the British Library. As the image on page 121 shows, the envelope in which Roger Keyes enclosed his letter to his wife, Eva, happily reveals that he survived the First World War and that Eva eventually read the letter at his request in 1944, after a long and happy marriage. Somewhat more tragically, Catherine Dickens carefully preserved the letters she had received from her husband, Charles, both before and after marriage, so that 'the world may know he loved me once'. One suspects that similar reasons might have prompted Mme Héger to reconstruct and preserve Charlotte Brontë's letters to her husband, Professor Héger.

Taken together, these love letters demonstrate that lovers' preoccupations have changed very little over the last 2,000 years, whatever the historical context. Feelings of joy, passion, jealousy and sadness, hope, longing, despair and contentment, ruled the human heart and mind, then as now. To read these carefully crafted survivals of the past in an age in which news and feelings seldom travel slowly in the post, will remind us that there is simply nothing quite like receiving a handwritten letter from the one you love.

'I and the child think of you always … I entreat you to return'

At the beginning of her letter, Isaias addresses Hephaestion as 'brother', probably by convention, though consanguineous marriages were not unknown in Egypt. It has been conjectured that Hephaestion was a soldier in the Egyptian army who, with a number of his comrades, had sought asylum in the Temple of Serapis at Memphis during the invasion of Egypt by the Syrian king, Antiochus Epiphanes. In July 168 BC Antiochus was forced to retire from Egypt, and at this point Hephaestion's wife, Isaias, would naturally have expected to be quickly reunited with her husband. Evidently, Hephaestion had still not returned home when Isaias was informed that he had been released from the Serapeum. Indignant, she wrote this letter, scolding him for deserting his family, informing him of the difficulties she had faced without him and entreating him to return home. She ended the letter with the softening clause: 'Please take care of yourself.' The letter, written on papyrus, was discovered in the temple, possibly left behind in haste when Hephaestion hurried home to his wife and child. 🖤

Isaias to her brother [husband] Hephaestion, greeting.

If you are well, and your affairs are prospering, it would be as I continually pray to the gods. I myself and the child and all the household are in good health and think of you always. When I received your letter from Horus, in which you explained that you were in sanctuary in the Serapeum at Memphis, I immediately gave thanks to the gods that you were well. But the fact that you did not return with all those who were shut up with you distresses me, for having steered myself and your child through such bad times, and having been

driven to the last extremity because of the high price of corn, I thought that now at least, with you at home, I should get some respite. But you have not given a thought to coming home nor given any regard to our circumstances, knowing how I was short of everything even before you left, not to mention how much time has since passed and such difficult times at that, during which you have sent nothing. And now that Horus, who has delivered your letter, has announced that you have been released, I am utterly distressed. Your mother is also anxious. For her sake as well as mine, I entreat you to please return to the city, unless something more urgent detains you. Please take care of yourself. Farewell.

]ϲΛϲ]ο̣ϲ̣ϲ̣ . . . ο̣ν̣ . . . ω̣ιΑΔΕΛ̣[

ϲιεϝϝωμ ϵ̣Ν̣τωιτ̣Δ̣ λ̣κατ̣Δ̣ τ̣Δ̣ . [

Δτ̣λαν̣τ̣Δλϵ̣ιτ̣ο̣ι αντοϲτ̣οιϲϲθϲοιϲ ϵυχ̣ο̣

ΝϵΝΗϲ̣υ̣λιτϵω̣ . κ̣η̣ . νη̣ϲϵϲ̣π̣ι . Δ̣ιν̣ο̣ν

Δ̣ . τϲ̣π̣ϲ̣ν̣ . ν̣ . ι̣ κ̣ϵ̣υ̣ . οι ϲ̣Δ̣ν̣ι̣κ̣ο̣ιτ̣ . π̣ . [

ϵ̣υ̣Δ̣ι̣Δτ̣Δ̣τ̣Η̣ . ιο̣ϲ κ̣α̣νϵ̣Δ̣ν̣τ̣ο̣ν . . . τϲ̣ . νο̣ι

κϵυ̣ι̣Δ̣λϵ̣ν̣Η̣ . ι̣ϲ̣ο̣ν̣τ̣ο̣ . ρ̣λ̣ο̣ . ϵ̣π̣ . ρ̣ο̣ . ο̣

τ̣Δ̣ρ̣μ̣ο̣ν ϵ̣ν̣Η̣ϲ̣ΔιϵΔ̣ϲϵι . . ϵ̣π̣Η̣ν̣

ϵΝ κ̣Δ̣τ̣ο̣χ̣Η̣Δ ϵ̣Ν̣τωιϲϝ̣Δ̣ρ̣Δ̣τ̣ϵ̣ι̣ωϲ̣ τ̣ο̣υ̣

ϵ̣ν̣τ̣ι̣ϲ̣μ̣ϵ̣ν̣ τ̣ω̣ιϲϝ̣ρ̣ω̣ϲ̣θϲ̣

ϵ̣τ̣ϲϵωϲ μ̣ο̣ι̣ϲθϲ̣ο̣ι̣ϲ ϵ̣υ̣χ̣Δ̣ρ̣ι̣ϲ̣τ̣ο̣υ̣ν̣

ϵ̣π̣ι̣Δϵ̣ . ω̣ι̣π̣ϲ̣τ̣ϲ̣Δ̣μ̣π̣Νϵϲ̣Δ̣ . ϲ̣ . ϲ̣ .

τ̣Δ̣ιΝ̣ϵ̣κ̣Δ̣λ̣τ̣ϵ̣ϲ̣ι̣ϲ̣ο̣ϲ̣ϲ̣ϲ̣ν̣ϲ̣ω̣ν̣τ̣ο̣λ̣ . μ̣ . ι̣ .

Δ̣λ̣ϲ̣ι̣ζ̣ο̣τ̣ω̣ν̣ ϵ̣ϲ̣κ̣Δ̣τ̣ο̣ϲ̣ ϵ̣κ̣τ̣ο̣τ̣τ̣ . ϲ̣ .

κ̣Η̣ρ̣ο̣ϲϵ̣υ̣Δ̣τ̣ο̣ι̣ . τ̣ . ϲ̣ϵ̣κ̣Δ̣ι̣ϲ̣ο̣τ̣ϲ̣Δ̣υ̣τ̣ . .

Δ̣ι̣λ̣κ̣ϵ̣κ̣τ̣ϲ̣ϝ̣Δ̣ν̣ι̣ϲ̣κ̣τ̣Δ̣κ̣Η̣ϵ̣ι̣ϲ̣τ̣ο̣Δ̣ν̣τ̣ι̣

ϵ̣κ̣Δ̣τ̣ο̣τ̣Δ̣ . Δ̣ι̣λ̣υ̣τ̣ο̣ν̣ ο̣τ̣ϵ̣ι̣ϵ̣τ̣ο̣τ̣ . ϲ̣π̣ . λ̣ο̣ν̣

κ̣Η̣Δ̣ι̣ . . . . τ̣ . Δ̣ϲ̣Ν̣ϵ̣τ̣ο̣ . ϵ̣π̣ο̣ . ϲ̣τ̣ . ϲ̣ .

τ̣ϵ̣τ̣ . ϲ̣ϵ̣ο̣π̣τ̣ . ϲ̣ϲ̣Δ̣Ν̣Δ̣ρ̣υ̣χ̣ι̣ϲ̣ϲ̣ ο̣ϲ̣λ̣ϲ̣

π̣τ̣Δ̣ . ϵ̣ . ϲ̣ . . ϲ̣ . κ̣Δ̣ . τ̣ο̣ι̣τ̣ο̣λ̣υ̣τ̣ϵ̣Ν̣ϵ̣ϲ̣ω̣ι̣

π̣Η̣ϲ̣ . ϵ̣Ν̣ϲ̣ϵ̣ο̣λ̣ο̣ϲ̣ . . ϲ̣Ν̣ϵ̣ι̣ϲ̣π̣ο̣Ν̣τ̣ο̣τ̣ϵ̣τ̣ϵ̣λ̣Δ̣ν̣τ̣Η̣τ̣

ϵ̣π̣ο̣τ̣ο̣ . . . . ϲ̣ . ο̣ρ̣ω̣ . ϲ̣ϵ̣Δ̣ϲ̣ο̣ϲ̣ο̣ν̣

ω̣ϲ̣ϵ̣π̣ . ϵ̣ϲ̣ο̣ . . ϲ̣ . τ̣ϵ̣τ̣ο̣κ̣ϲ̣τ̣ρ̣ . ο̣ν̣ϵ̣ . ϲ̣ϵ̣Δ̣Δ̣ο̣ν̣

τ̣Η̣ϲ̣ο̣π̣τ̣ϵ̣ . τ̣ϵ̣ο̣ . ϲ̣ . ρ̣ο̣χ̣ . ρ̣ . ρ̣ϵ̣Δ̣π̣ο̣τ̣ϵ̣τ̣ο̣λ̣ . . ϲ̣ .

κ̣Η̣ϲ̣τ̣ο̣τ̣ . τ̣ . ι̣ϝ̣ϵ̣ι̣ρ̣ο̣ν̣τ̣Η̣ϲ̣ϵ̣ν̣τ̣ο̣ . ο̣ϲ̣τ̣ϵ̣ω̣τ̣ϲ̣ .

ϵ̣π̣ο̣Δ̣ϵ̣ . ο̣μ̣ϲ̣ τ̣ο̣τ̣ϵ̣τ̣Δ̣Η̣ ϵ̣π̣τ̣ϲ̣ϝ̣ο̣λ̣Η̣ν̣τ̣ο̣φ̣Δ̣κ̣ϵ̣υ̣

τ̣ο̣ι̣κ̣ . . . ϲ̣ϵ̣Δ̣ι̣τ̣ο̣τ̣ . κ̣Δ̣τ̣ο̣ϲ̣ π̣ι̣ϲ̣ϵ̣τ̣τ̣ . τ̣ο̣λ̣ϲ̣ϲ̣ϲ̣ .

ϵ̣κ̣τ̣Η̣ϲ̣ . κ̣Δ̣τ̣ο̣χ̣Η̣ϲ̣τ̣ο̣τ̣ο̣ν̣ . Δ̣ . ω̣ι̣Δ̣λ̣ϲ̣ι̣ζ̣ο̣τ̣Η̣ν̣

υ̣τ̣Η̣ν̣ο̣υ̣ . . ϲ̣ . Δ̣τ̣ . Δ̣ κ̣Η̣τ̣ο̣ . κ̣ο̣ϲ̣τ̣τ̣ο̣τ̣ . ϲ̣τ̣ . ο̣ν̣ .

. ο̣ρ̣ϵ̣τ̣ϲ̣ϵ̣κ̣τ̣ο̣τ̣ . ϲ̣ϲ̣ . . . . ϲ̣ο̣ι̣ϲ̣Δ̣τ̣ϵ̣ι̣κ̣Δ̣λ̣Δ̣ρ̣τ̣ο̣

. ν̣Δ̣ι̣ϲ̣ϲ̣ϵ̣ρ̣ο̣ . . . . ϲ̣ . τ̣ . ϵ̣υ̣ . ϵ̣ι̣ϲ̣ϵ̣Δ̣π̣τ̣ο̣ . ϲ̣ . ϲ̣ν̣ϵ̣ .

Δ̣ν̣Δ̣ϝ̣κ̣ . . Δ̣ . ϵ̣ . . . . . . ϲ̣ . ϲ̣ϲ̣ . . . ϵ̣ι̣Δ̣χ̣Δ̣ . ϵ̣ϲ̣ϵ̣λ̣Δ̣ι̣τ̣

. ω̣μ̣Δ̣ . ϲ̣ϵ̣ν̣π̣ι̣ . μ̣ϵ̣ . . . . . τ̣ . ν̣ . . ϲ̣ . ϲ̣λ̣Δ̣λ̣ . χ̣ .

Right reverent and worshipfull husband...

whech I beseche almyghty god long...

in good heele of body ney of herte...

I day it not [..]. And my lady...

of for the whech god knoweth I...

hade not halfe the lyvelode that...

me to kepe my tyme whey old go, I...

say that I do dnye ye shall not...

be now so wroth I tryst it shall...

kepyng And I beseche zow that...

at tyngest in full hony herte...

Feb. 1476.7.   16 E.iv.

'My heart bids me ever more to love you, truly over all earthly thing'

The 'Paston letters' are the most famous surviving collection of private correspondence from fifteenth-century England. Over one thousand in number, and dating from 1420 to the end of the fifteenth century, the letters present an incomparable picture of middle-class life during one of the most turbulent periods in English history. Although they are primarily business letters, some deal with courtship and marriage.

In this famous letter, Margery Brews reveals the depth of her love for John Paston III, whom she addresses as 'my right well-beloved Valentine', and expresses  her sorrow at the bitter family dispute over the size of her dowry. For although Margery Brews, daughter of Sir Thomas Brews, came from a distinguished family, the match between her and John was embittered by her father's demand for a richer dowry than John had intended to offer. All obstacles were eventually overcome when John's mother, Margaret Paston, gave the couple the manor of Sparham, and the marriage took place before the end of 1477. A decade later, John Paston III fought at the battle of Stoke to defend the new Tudor dynasty against the promoters of the pretender, Lambert Simnel, and was knighted on the field. John and Margery's eldest son, William, born in 1478, was also knighted and became a prominent figure at the court of Henry VIII. 🍃

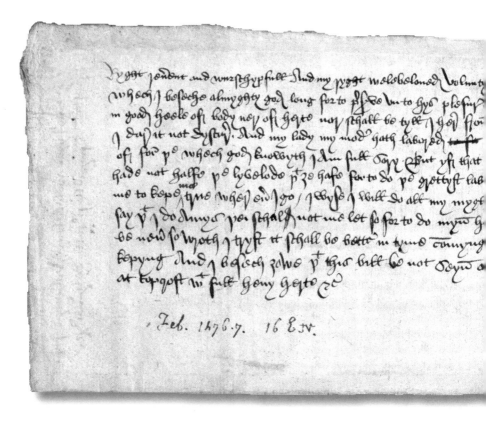

Right Reverend and worshipful and my right well-beloved Valentine,
I recommend me unto you full heartily, desiring to hear of your welfare, which
I beseech Almighty God long to preserve unto His pleasure and your heart's
desire. And if it please you to hear of my welfare, I am not in good health either
of body or heart, nor shall I be till I hear from you for there knows no creature
what pain I endure. And even on pain of death I dare it not reveal. And my lady
my mother has pressed the matter on my father full diligently, but she can no
more get than you know of, for which God knows I am most sorry. But if you love
me, as I trust verily you do, you will not leave me therefore. For if you had not

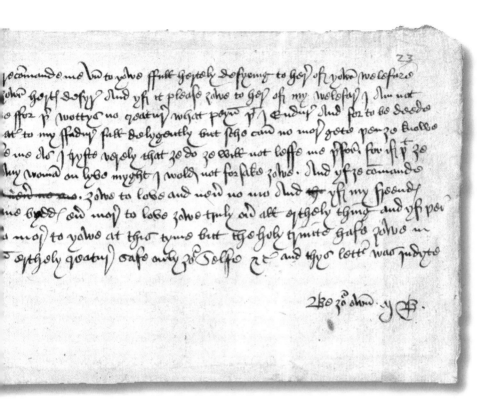

half the livelihood that you have, and if I had to do the greatest labour that any woman alive might, I would not forsake you. And if you command me to keep me true wherever I go I will do all my might to love you and no one else. And if my friends say that I do amiss they shall not hinder me from doing so. My heart bids me ever more to love you, truly over all earthly thing. And if they be never more angry, I trust it shall be better in time coming. No more to you at this time, but the Holy Trinity have you in keeping. And I beseech you that this letter be not seen by any earthly creature save only yourself. And this letter was written at Topcroft with full heavy heart.   *By your own M. B.*

...gratum... vias subi... teneor / quippe
a procrastinatio vestri ad me adventus. Habeo
quod huic meo tam ardenti in se amori, tam amaute
oro ut cepit / et sicuti ego sum noctes et dies
uoque et ipsa meum recens nomine in suo semper pectore
tu maturet: ut ex absentibus simus presentes: et con /
serata gaudia suos aliquando fructus decerpat.
ritas innuxit) tu exequtus in commendanda scilicet
te parentibus meis / atque in declaranda filiali vestra
quidem fuit illis pergratum audire (me potius /
que obsecro vestre quoque Celsitudini mutuas in hoc
dere: et Serenissimis. Dominis meis unis parentibus me
. eos aut non secus quam si mei proprii parentes
or. et obsequo. atque illis feliciora et prospera cuncta
tas felix et fausta sit. Leta quoque sese servet et
crebro et sepe me visere velit. Quod est futur
Castello meo Ludlo iij Nonas Octob. Anno. 1499

amantissimus Sponsus ⊨ —— Arthurus princeps ⊨
Wallie Dux Cornubie et Rethuis primogenitus

'And let your coming to me be hastened, that instead of being absent we may be present with each other'

In August 1497, the ten-year old Prince Arthur, eldest son of King Henry VII and Elizabeth of York, was formally betrothed to Katherine of Aragon, daughter of Ferdinand and Isabella of Spain. The marriage by proxy took place at the ancient palace of Woodstock in Oxfordshire, with the Spanish ambassador, Pedro de Ayala, standing in for the bride. Katherine was due to travel to England in 1499, but her departure was delayed by disputes between Henry VII and Ferdinand over the payment of her dowry and by the insecurity of the Tudor dynasty. This is one of several love letters that Arthur sent to Katherine, his 'dearest spouse'. Writing in Latin, Arthur thanked her for her sweet letters and confessed an earnest desire to see her: 'let your coming to me be hastened, that instead of being absent we may be present with each other, and the love conceived between us and the wished-for joys may reap their proper fruit'. Two more years, however, were to elapse before Katherine would travel to England and Arthur would meet his bride-to-be. They were eventually married in Old St Paul's Cathedral on 14 November 1501. Five months later, Arthur, a weak and sickly boy, died at the age of fifteen. Katherine would remain in England to become the wife of his brother Henry, the future Henry VIII – a union that would have the most profound consequences for both the king and England. ❦

Most illustrious and most excellent lady, my dearest spouse, I wish you very much health, with my hearty commendation.

    I have read the most sweet letters of your Highness lately given to me, from which I have easily perceived your most entire love to me. Truly, your letters, traced by your own hand, have so delighted me, and have rendered me so cheerful and jocund, that I fancied I beheld your Highness and conversed with and embraced my dearest wife. I cannot tell you what an earnest desire I feel to see your Highness, and how vexatious to me is this procrastination about your coming. I owe eternal thanks to your excellence that you so lovingly correspond to this my most ardent love. Let it continue, I entreat, as it has begun; and, like I cherish your sweet remembrance night and day, so do you preserve my name ever fresh in your breast. And let your coming to me be hastened, that instead of being absent we may be present with each other, and the love conceived between us and the wished-for joys may reap their proper fruit.

Moreover I have done as your illustrious Highness enjoined me, that is to say, in commending you to the most serene lord and lady King and Queen my parents, and in declaring your filial regard towards them, which to them was most pleasing to hear, especially from my lips. I also beseech your Highness that it may please you to exercise a similar good office for me and to commend me with hearty good will to my most serene lord and lady your parents; for I greatly value, venerate, and esteem them, even as though they were my own, and wish them all happiness and prosperity.

May your Highness be ever fortunate and happy, and be kept safe and joyful, and let me know it often and speedily by your letters, which will be to me most joyous.

Your Highness' loving spouse, Arthur, Prince of Wales,
Duke of Cornwall, & Eldest son of the King.
Ludlow Castle, October 5, 1499

'... you who since my childhood I have always wanted to love, serve, esteem and honour'

This charming 'little book of love' is one of the most personal and intimate manuscripts to have survived from the Renaissance. It was commissioned in about 1500 by Pierre Sala, a courtier and man of letters from Lyons, as a love-token for Marguerite Bullioud. Pierre and Marguerite had in fact been childhood sweethearts, but went on to marry other people. By 1500, however, they were both widowed and so Sala conceived the book, as he explains in its dedicatory letter, to offer to Marguerite as a symbol of his desire to regain her heart. The rest of the volume consists of a collection of love poems that Sala wrote for her, and then had embellished by an artist. The first miniature is the most personal illustration in the manuscript. It depicts Sala placing his heart inside a marguerite flower in the centre of a bed of pansies (pensées), symbols of thoughts and dreams. Sala's accompanying verse reads: 'My heart wishes to be in this marguerite; it will be there despite what envious persons may say; it will always be in my thoughts because it is the queen of flowers.' Beneath the verse, the initial M of Marguerite is formed from a pair of draughtsman's compasses, the traditional symbol of Renaissance lovers. Pierre Sala and Marguerite Bullioud were finally married in around 1515–19; meanwhile the manuscript continues to bear testament to their enduring love. 🍒

To you my dearest and most honoured lady, Madame […], you who since my childhood I have always wanted to love, serve, esteem and honour to the best of my ability more than any other lady alive for the great qualities you possess, as the most illustrious and most perfect, she who, in my opinion, has always surpassed all others in feeling, honour and worth, since in your person are to be found all the fine qualities one could wish for in a woman. Your most humble and loyal servant, who forever wishes to consider you as his sole lady and

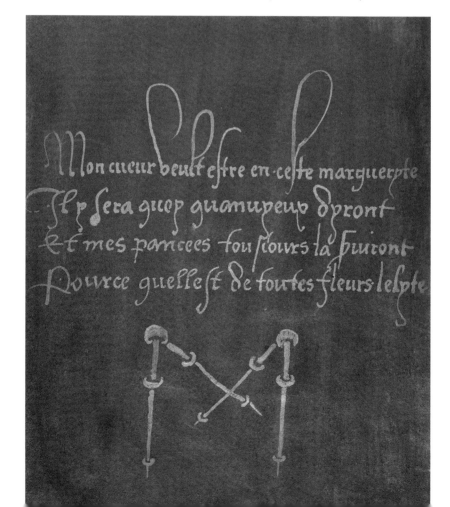

mistress with all his heart and as humbly as is possible, commends himself to your kindly grace, informing you that the great sweetnesses, beauties and courtesies with which your noble body is replete are constantly before his eyes or in his thoughts; therein they obstinately remain and for this reason he is constantly reopening and aggravating the incurable wound you inflicted upon him in the past, from which

he cannot be healed and which leads him to endure and suffer much sorrow and pain – suffering he gladly bears most uncomplainingly and patiently since it comes from you from whom he would rather receive pain and torment than pleasure and joy from any other, because you alone are his succour, his well-being and his nourishment; you are the only medicine which can cure him if you so wish. […] Therefore I clench my hands and beseech you, my sole lady and mistress, that my situation which is so pitiful be restored and swiftly remedied by your feeling lest you long repent it. And, in order to refresh your memory, I am sending you this little book containing pictures and words which are the two ways by which we can enter the house of memory, since pictures are for the eye, and words are for the ear, and both make past things seem as if they were present. And thus, since by means of these two things we can make present what is absent, and since in the course of the long period of waiting of which you are the cause, your good servant has somewhat lost track of this noblest memory, may these pictures and words put him back on the path so surely that he might never leave it again.

'Be daily prove you shall me find To be to you both loving and kind'

With the exception of Henry VIII's love letters to Anne Boleyn, now held in the Vatican Library, this Book of Hours provides one of the most evocative pieces of evidence for Henry's love affair with Anne. Produced in around 1500, this sumptuously illustrated devotional text was presented to the British Museum in 1823 by King George IV as part of the library of King George III. Very little is known for certain about the manuscript's previous ownership, but, in light of the intimate nature of the notes that Henry and Anne wrote in it to each other, it seems very likely that it did once belong to Anne. Henry chose to write his note to Anne on a page depicting the man of sorrows, thereby intentionally presenting himself as the lovesick king. He wrote in French: 'If you remember my love in your prayers as strongly as I adore you, I shall scarcely be forgotten, for I am yours. Henry Rex forever.' Anne responded with a couplet in English: 'Be daily prove you shall me find / To be to you both loving and kind.' Anne's choice of page was also highly significant, for she wrote her message below an image of the Annunciation, with the Archangel Gabriel telling the Virgin Mary that she would bear a son. By association, Anne was telling Henry that she would succeed where his first queen, Katherine of Aragon, had failed and provide him with the son and heir that he so desperately longed for. 🍎

Se filon mon affection la suffenate sera
en voz prieres ne feray et ces oplie
car ie le fuis HENRY · Th · a Jamays

*If you remember my love in your prayers as strongly as
I adore you, I shall scarcely be forgotten, for I am yours.
Henry Rex forever.*

*Be daily prove you shall me find
To be to you both loving and kind.*
(Anne Boleyn)

...secretes my frede these wordes not to be only
...t moost truely impressed in the hert, muche...
...come to go aboute to prayse my self, or ascrybe...
to do I mynde nothyng lesse, but a playne symple...
...tabe towarde your maiestye procedyng, the from...
...wherin I must nedes confesse I deserve no...
...havyng suche Juste occasion to do the...
...wythe your maiestye, as I do wythe god for...
...heped upon me dayly, knowlegyng my self...
...nto hym in that I do omytt my dutye towarde...
...to recompense the leste of thy benefytes, in nye...
...bure to dye, but yett I hope in gracyous accept...
...And even suche confidence I have in your...
...vyng my self never to have done my dutye...
...te to suche a noble and worthy prynce, at... that
...and receyved so muche love and kyndnes, which...
...yt; left I sholde be to tedyouse unto your maiestye,
...letter, comyttyng you in to the governance of the lorde
...felycite here, and after thys lyf to enioy the kyngdome of...

By your maiesties humble
obedyent lovyng wyfe and
servant   Kateryn the Qwene KP

'God, the knower of secrets, can judge these words not to be only written with ink, but most truly impressed in the heart'

Henry VIII wed Katherine Parr on 12 July 1543 at Hampton Court Palace, in the presence of his three children, Mary, Elizabeth and Edward. Henry was not the twice-widowed Katherine's personal choice, for she was already in love with the younger and more exciting Thomas Seymour, brother of Henry's third wife, Jane. Nevertheless, Katherine bravely put duty before love and became Henry's sixth and last wife. In July 1544, Henry left the shores of England for his final military expedition to France. Shortly before sailing he appointed Katherine, his bride of barely a year, Queen Regent during his absence. This letter, written to Henry by Katherine after his departure, indicates that their marriage had already grown to be very loving and affectionate. Full of heartfelt pleas for news of the king, Katherine tells Henry that she longs for his presence even though she understands that his absence is necessary. Towards the end of the letter, in order to explain her absolute and submissive love for Henry, the devoutly Protestant queen compares it with her love for God. Just a few months after Henry's death in 1547, Thomas Seymour eventually became Katherine's fourth husband, but Katherine tragically died in 1548, soon after giving birth to their first child. ❦

Although the discourse of time and account of days neither is long nor many of your Majesty's absence, yet the want of your presence, so much beloved and desired of me, maketh me that I cannot quietly pleasure in anything until I hear from your Majesty. The time, therefore, seemeth to me very long, with a great desire to know how your highness hath done since your departing hence, whose prosperity and health I prefer and desire more than mine own. And whereas I know your Majesty's absence is never without great respects of things most convenient and necessary, yet love and affection compelleth me to desire your presence.

And again, the same zeal and love forces me also to be best content with that which is your will and pleasure. And thus love maketh me in all things to set apart mine own commodity and pleasure, and to embrace most joyfully his will and pleasure whom I love. God, the knower of secrets, can judge these words not to be only written with ink, but most truly impressed in the heart. Much more I omit, lest I should seem to go about to praise myself, or crave a thank; which thing to do I mind nothing less, but a plain, simple relation of my zeal and love toward your Majesty, proceeding from the abundance

of the heart. Wherein I must needs confess I deserve no worthy commendation, having such just occasion to do the same.

I make like account with your Majesty, as I do with God for his benefits and gifts heaped upon me daily, acknowledging myself always a great debtor unto him in that I do omit my duty toward him, not being able to recompense the least of his benefits; in which state I am certain and sure to die, but yet I hope in His gracious acceptation of my goodwill. And even such confidence I have in your Majesty's gentleness, knowing myself never to have done my duty as was requisite and mete to such a noble and worthy prince, at whose hands I have found and received so much love and goodness, that with words I cannot express it. Lest I should be too tedious unto your Majesty, I finish this my scribbled letter, committing you into the governance of the Lord with long life and prosperous felicity here, and after this life to enjoy the kingdom of his elect.

From Greenwich, by your Majesty's humble, obedient, loving wife and servant,

Kateryn the Queen.

lesse. Therfore for the honor
ffell constant in kindnes, for all
are confest to be perfect. and so
receaue all wishes of perfect

r Maties most humble
ffaythfull and affectionate
seruant.

'... the two windows of your privy chamber shall be the poles of my sphere'

Robert Devereux, 2nd Earl of Essex and stepson of Queen Elizabeth I's favourite, Robert Dudley, Earl of Leicester, first arrived at court in 1584. Within three years the dashing twenty-one-year-old had become Elizabeth's constant companion and reigning favourite at court. At the outset of their relationship it was observed that he 'cometh not to his own lodging til the birds sing in the morning'. In 1587 Essex replaced Leicester as Master of the Horse and over the next decade he obtained several important military offices. It was his failure, however, as Lord Lieutenant of Ireland to suppress Tyrone's revolt that led to Essex being stripped of all his offices and placed under house arrest. Angry at his humiliation, Essex led a rash rebellion that resulted in his being charged with treason and executed on Tower Hill on 25 February 1601. This is one of an extraordinary collection of forty-three remarkably intimate letters from Essex to Elizabeth that chart the course of their relationship from 1590 until Essex's death. Written in October 1591, it dates from the period of his greatest favour with the queen. Following courtly convention of the time, Essex assumes the role of Elizabeth's lover, lamenting his separation from his royal mistress while commanding the queen's army in France, and vows that 'the two windows of your privy chamber shall be the poles of my sphere where, as long as your Majesty will please to have me, I am fixed and unmovable'. 🍐'

Most fayre, most deare, and most excellent
soueraigne. the first sute I make unto y
Ma.tie upon my arriuall, is that y Ma.tie will
free me from writing to y of any matter of
busines. my duty shallbe otherwise performd
by aduertising my L.L. of y Ma.ties commaunds of
all thinges here: and yett my affection nott
wronged w.th hills me shall zealous fayth
and humble kindnes are argum enough for
a letter. att my departure I had a resolue to
humbly to disingage myself from this french action
in my absence I conceaue an assured hope to
do somthing that shall make me worthy of
the name of y seruant. att my returne I
will humbly beseach y Ma.tie that no cause
butt a greatt action of y owne may draw m
out of y sight. for the 2 windowes of y
privy chamber shallbe the poles of my
sphere. who, as long as y Ma.tie will pleas
to haue me, I am fixed and unmoueable.
when y thinke that heauen to good for m
I will nott fall like a starr, butt be con
like a vapor by the same sun that dre
me up to such a height. while y Ma.tie
gyues me leaue to say I loue y, my fort
is as my affection unmatchable. if euer
y deny me that libertye y may end m
lyfe, butt neuer shake my constancy. for w
the sweetnes of y nature turned into th
greatest bitternes shall itt be. yt is no
in y power, (as greatt a Q. as y are) to

Letter from the
Earl of Essex to
Elizabeth I,
18 October 1591

make me loue y [selfe] & [therefore] for the honor
of y sex, show y selfe constant in kindnes, for all
y other vertues are [confest] so to perfecth. and so
I beseach y [Madie] receiue all wishes of perfect
happines from

y [Ma]ties most humble
[faithfull] and affectionate
[seruant].

Most fair, most dear, and most excellent sovereign. The first suit I make unto
your Majesty upon my arrival, is that your Majesty will free me from writing
to you of any matter of business. My duty shall be otherwise performed by
advertising my Lords of your Majesty's counsel of all things here; and yet my
affection not wronged which tells me that zealous faith and humble kindness
are argument enough for a letter. At my departure I had a restless desire honestly
to disengage myself from this French action. In my absence I conceive an assured
hope to do something that shall make me worthy of the name of your servant.
At my return I will humbly beseech your Majesty that no cause but a great
action of your own may draw me out of your sight. For the two windows of your
privy chamber shall be the poles of my sphere where, as long as your Majesty
will please to have me, I am fixed and unmovable. When you think that heaven

too good for me, I will not fall like a star, but be consumed like a vapour by the same sun that drew me up to such a height. While your Majesty gives me leave to say I love you, my fortune is as my affection, unmatchable. If ever you deny me that liberty you may end my life, but never shake my constancy, for were the sweetness of your nature turned into the greatest bitterness that could be, it is not in your power (as great a Queen as you are) to make me love you less. Therefore, for the honour of your sex, show yourself constant in kindness, for all your other virtues are confessed to be perfect and so I beseech your Majesty receive all wishes of perfect happiness from

Your Majesty's most humble, faithful and affectionate servant, Essex. Dieppe, this 18th October

...d a bodye, for the rest, y gesse
the y am seperated In body farr
yett y leave the better parte of m
..tend thee, wch y know In being
..ourly saluting off the will doe the
...west male and thinke y pray
..the cannott kepe me Longe for
kissing thy hands more then
.t 29 of August.

he who being absent from
the is nott wth himselfe

Tho: Balkervile

'And so I leave thee, kissing thy hands more than a thousand times'

By the time of his appointment in 1595 as military commander on Sir John Hawkins and Sir Francis Drake's ill-fated expedition to the Indies, Sir Thomas Baskerville had enjoyed a distinguished military career. He had served as a captain in the Netherlands under Robert Dudley, Earl of Leicester, and was knighted in recognition of the part he played in the capture of *Bergen op Zoom* in 1588. Before setting sail from Plymouth, Baskerville wrote this letter to his wife, Mary, to inform her of his imminent departure and to warn her not to expect to hear from him until his return. Full of optimism, he told her of their plan to capture the principal galleon of the Spanish treasure-fleet, which had been disabled and was lying at Puerto Rico. The expedition, however, was disastrous almost from the start: Sir John Hawkins fell ill and died at sea off Puerto Rico; the Spaniards were forewarned and the attack failed; and Drake, after a succession of further failures, fell ill with dysentery and died off Porto Bello, Panama, on 28 January 1596. Baskerville buried him at sea and brought the remnants of the expedition back to England. In 1597 Mary accompanied her husband on his last voyage to France, where he died of a fever, just two months after the birth of their first son, Hannibal Baskerville. Thomas Baskerville was buried in the new choir of St Paul's Cathedral, beneath a monument that was destroyed in the Great Fire of London in 1666. 🐚

Sweet Malle, I have now received two letters from thee and answered thee none, but now I will come out of this debt. Thy cousin Chachme I have entertained, who for thy sake (who hath all power of me) I will use as well as my means or fortune will give me leave. We attend only the wind, and therefore you must take this letter as a farewell, for I trust I shall have no opportunity to write to you

more till my return, which I hope shall be in six months or seven at the farthest, but longer than eight I will not take of you, therefore about that time assuredly look for our return. We have received advice that hath put great hopes into us, and that is of a ship beaten into an island in the West Indies by tempest, laden with two millions and a half, which I doubt not by God's help to carry. I leave then to thy judgement whether it be not six months well spent to get such a booty. For the rest, I give thee full assurance that though I am separated in body far from thee by great distance, yet I leave the better part of me, which is my spirit, to attend thee, which I know in bearing the continual company and hourly saluting of thee will do the part of a friend. Farewell, sweet Malle, and think, I pray thee, that my desire to see thee cannot keep me long from thee. And so I leave thee, kissing thy hands more than a thousand times. Plymouth, this 21 of August.

> *He who being absent from thee is not with himself,*
> *Thomas Baskerville*

Swett malle I hate now receaved 2 letters from the and answered the ~~14~~

~~till now~~, butt now I will com owt of this ditt, this coussen Chassine

I have entertayned ~~and~~ for thy sake (who hatte all powre off me) I will

Use as well as my meanes or fortune will geve me leave, we

atend only the wind, and therfor you must take this letter as afarewell

for I trust I shall have no opertunity to wryght to you more

till my retourne ꝯ I hope shalbe In sip, monithe or seven att

the farthist, butt lenger then ᵱ I willnott take off you, therfor

abowte thatt tyme assuridly loke for our retourne, we have receaved

advise thatt have grett dreatt hopes Into 33, and thatt is off asshipe

taken Into an Iland In the west Indies by tempest laden w

20 millions and ahalfe, ꝯ I dought nott by gods helpe butt to

carriie, I leave then to thy Judgmeant whither yt be nott sip

enoughe well spent to gett Into a botye, for the rest I geve

thee full assurance thatt thoughe I am seperated In body farr

from thee by great distance, yett I have the better parte off me

ꝯ Is my spyritt I leave to atend thee, ꝯ I know In being

the continuall company and howrly saluting off the will doe the

parte of afrind farwell swett malle and thinke I pray

the thatt my desire to see the cannott kepe me longe from

the and so I leave the kissing thy hands more then

a 1000 times plymuthe this 27 of August

he who being absent from
the is nott w him selfe –

J Thos Baskerville

I haue been t[...]
bedde and han[...]
yonto choose which you like
to the patonr[...]
you lack any t[...]
company you [...]
me knowe of [...]
yonrs the rest[...]
Intreating th[...]
the more merry to think then [...]
had rather b[...]
place vnder [...]

Honborn 26
Nobe: 1622.

'I am forced yet to send the shadow of myself'

Thomas Knyvett of Ashwellthorpe in Norfolk, a direct descendant of Sir John Knyvett, Chancellor of Richard III, married Katherine Burgh, the youngest daughter of Thomas Burgh, 5th Baron of Gainsborough, at Mary-le-Strand in London on 28 February 1620. The couple experienced frequent periods of separation throughout their marriage: in the earlier years on account of legal business that demanded Knyvett's presence in London and, following the outbreak of the Civil War, due to difficulties with the Parliamentary government in which his Royalist sympathies involved him. During his absences from home, Knyvett wrote regularly to Katherine; eighty-eight of his letters have survived, revealing the deep affection between husband and wife that helped them to weather the difficulties and dangers which they faced. Knyvett wrote this letter a year and a half into their marriage, but his affectionate words, his declared impatience to return to Katherine's side and to sleep in her arms, and reference to his careful choice of presents for his wife are all regular features of the other letters. Katherine died at the end of April 1646. Knyvett outlived his wife by more than ten years but did not remarry, and instead focused on finding suitable marriage partners for their four surviving children. He was buried alongside Katherine in 1658 in Ashwellthorpe church. 🍂

Sweet heart, I am forced yet to send the shadow of myself, the true affection of a substance that loves you above all the world. My business I hope will be effectually dispatched presently, and God willing I will be with thee before you are aware. I have been to look for stuff for your bed and have sent down patterns for you to choose which you like best, they are the nearest to the pattern that we can find. If you lack anything except my company you are to blame not to let me know of it, for myself being only yours the rest do follow. Thus in haste, entreating thee to be merry, and the more merry to think thou have him in thy arms that had rather be with you than in any place under heaven. And so I rest

*Thy dear loving
husband forever,
Thomas Knyvett.*

Sweet harte I ame forst ~~to~~ yet to send the
shaddowe of my selfe, the true affection
of a substance that loves you above all
the world, my busines I hope wilbe effectually dispatch presently and god willing
I will be with the before you are aware
I have been to ~~too~~ look for stufe for y
bedde and have sent downe ~~paternes~~ for
yanto choose which you like best, thay are the neerest
to ~~the~~ patourne that ~~that~~ wee can finde; if
you lack any thing ~~to my~~ accept my
company you are to blame not ~~to lett~~
me ~~knowe~~ of it, for my selfe being only
yours the rest doe ~~followe~~, thus in hast
Intreating the to be ~~not~~ merry and
the more merry ~~to~~ think thou hast him in thy armes that
had rather be with you then in any
place under heaven, and so I rest

Honborn 26
9obe: 1622.

Thy dear loving
husband forever

Tho: Knybett

My deve dad and Gos

for imitation of s.d fa[...]
an account of him yo[...]
obedient stout kind [...]
s.d [illegible] were yo[...]
perfectie reconered
three things that
this great busines [...]
for yours [illegible] you
nations honor[...]
my selfe that tho[...]
[...] last ver[...]

'I have too lately said I love you better than myself'

As both King James VI of Scotland and later as King of England, James I's sexuality and choice of male partners were the subject of gossip from the taverns to the Privy Council. When James inherited the English throne from Queen Elizabeth I in 1603, it was openly joked that '*Rex fuit Elizabeth: nunc est regina Jacobus*' ('Elizabeth was King: now James is Queen'). George Villiers, the son of an impoverished Leicestershire squire, was introduced to the king in the summer of 1614 and in November that year he was appointed the Royal Cupbearer. The following year he was knighted and appointed Gentleman of the Bedchamber and in 1616 created Viscount Villiers. Responding to his Privy Council's remonstrations in 1617, after having elevated Villiers to the earldom of Buckingham, James declared that that he loved Buckingham 'more than any other man'. The king continued to delight in his favourite, whose spectacular rise continued, becoming a Marquis in 1618, Lord High Admiral in 1619 and finally the Duke of Buckingham in 1623. In the same year Buckingham wrote this letter to James from Madrid, where he was engaged in marriage negotiations for Prince Charles, the king's son, to marry a Spanish princess. He addressed the king as 'My dear Dad and Gossip' (chum) and signed himself 'your majesty's humble slave and dog Steenie'. Steenie was James I's nickname for him, a diminutive of Stephen and a Biblical reference to St Stephen, whose face at the moment of martyrdom was said to have been that of an angel. 🐛

My dear Dad and Gossip,

In imitation of St. John I will give you an account of him you love best after your obedient, stout, kind and discreet son: that's myself. Sir, I assure you I am now so perfectly recovered that there is but three things that troubles me. First, that this great business hath no better an issue for yours, your son's, and whole nation's honour; but in this I comfort myself that though it's late, yet now at last you shall know the truth and know what to trust hereafter to. The second is my absence from you, but in that I have likewise comfort that now I shall be soon with you. The third and last was weariness with looking and casting what presents to give here away; but the pleasure I have now in writing to your Majesty hath also relieved me of that, so that now I want nothing but means how to appear in some degree thankful and worthy of your absent favours. But this is not a work of a newly recovered man out of a sickness; it rather requires a man in perfect health and strength and likely to live hundreds of years. Therefore, my best way is to make much of myself that I may live longer, and methinks I hear you say I thank thee more for that than for service to myself. If the substance of this letter be naught or little worth, I am sure my intentions good and so is the form, for with the same style I began I end: that is, in confidence and love. Yet in one respect

I should be discouraged to do so, for though you are the best father, master, and I may with sauciness put in friend, though it be with an humble heart, yet when I consider my own defects and unworthiness and how fruitless a servant I have been, it makes me with shame and admiration look both on your Majesty and your servant. Before Clarke came, I had thrown off sickness, but the relations he made of your abundant care of me, and largely expressed in a letter from Secretary Conway, hath made me take a full possession of health, so that though your favours may say truly in loving you

I love myself, yet the ambition I shall ever have of preserving them with the loss of life and all other things I have, shall witness I love you with more than a self-love. Sir, judge whether I have pleasure or not in writing to you, for though I thought to have made an end on the other side, methinks it's too soon here; but I fear I have troubled you too long. And I have too lately said I love you better than myself, so in writing longer to please myself, I should give to what I have already said a contradiction, wherefore I'll end with craving your blessing.

The nine and twentieth
of August

Your Majesty's humble
slave and dog,
Steenie

My deve dad and Gossope

In imitation of St fisher I will giue you
an account of him you loue best that my selfe
obedient stout kind and discreet sonne
Sr ... assewre you I ame now so
... reconered that there is but
three things that troubles me first that
this great busines hath no better an issue
for your ... your somis and whole
nations honor but in this I comfort
my selfe that though its late yett
now at last you shall know the
treuth and know what to trust
hereafter to, the second is my absence
from you but in that I haue lkwise
comfort that now I shall be some
with you, the third and lost
was werines with conkeins and casting
what presents to giue deue away but
the pleasure I haue now in wishing
your mats hath alle releued me of
that, so that now I want nothing but
meanes how to aspire ... in some degre

First and last pages of letter from George Villiers to James I, 29 August 1623

your seruant, before Clarke came I
had throne of sicknes but the relations
he made of your aboundant care of me
and largelie exprest in a letter from
secretarie Coneway hath made me
take a full posseshion of ~~them~~ helth, so
that though your fauors may say treulie
in loueing you I loue my selfe yett the
ambition I shall euer of preseuing them with
~~neuer~~ the poss. of life and all other things
I haue shall wittnes I loue you with
more then a selfe loue, sr iudge whe=
ther I haue pleasure or not in writeing
to you for though I thought to
haue made an end on the other side
me thinks its to sone here, but I fee
I haue trowbled you to longe, and I
haue now latelie saide I loue you
better then my selfe so my writeing longer
to pleas my selfe I should giue to what
I haue alredie said a contridiction
wherfore Ile end with crauening your

the nine and twentith
of august

blessing

your maj. humble
slaue, and doge
steenie

aversion and I should sooner hope to gain
one then upon one that did not consider mee
or hate
love mee; ile swere she is much Easyr to
bee, there are a great many ingredien
aking mee happy in a husband first a
and to bee that he
our humors must agree must hau
ng that I haue had and vsed that kinde of co
st not bee soe much a Country Gentleman
ing but hawks and dog's and bee fonder of
them
vse, nor the next sort of
then
nor further to bee Justice of peace and
Sheriff who read noe book but statut's
but how to make a speech enterlarded
ay amaze his disagreeing poore Neighbo
them
ter then perswade into quietnesse; hee must
began the world in a free scoole was sent
vniversity and is at his farthest when he
Court has noe acquaintance but those of
e places speaks the french hee has pick
d admires nothing but the story's hee has
t were kept there before his Time; hee
llant neither that liues in a Tauern and a
t imagin how an howre should bee spent
se it bee in sleeping that makes court to all t

'... there are a great many ingredients must go to the making me happy in a husband'

During their lengthy courtship, Dorothy, daughter of Sir Peter Osborne, royalist lieutenant-governor of Guernsey, wrote a well-known sequence of over seventy letters to Sir William Temple, son of Sir John Temple, Master of the Rolls in Ireland. Having first met in 1646, when William was due to embark on a five-year tour of the continent, their correspondence finally commenced in the winter of 1652 when William was abroad on a diplomatic mission, and ended in October 1654 when Dorothy was struck down by a severe attack of smallpox that nearly killed her. All kinds of practical difficulties beset the couple. Both families opposed their engagement, due to personal antipathies intensified by opposing political views. Dorothy's father had also hoped for a more lucrative match for his youngest daughter to help restore the family fortunes, which had suffered due to the heavy fines imposed by the parliamentary government for his support for Charles I.

At last, however, all obstacles were surmounted, and the pair married on Christmas Day in 1654. In this letter written the previous year, Dorothy provides William with her definition of the perfect husband. As with all her letters, it is elegantly written and full of a tenderness, vivaciousness and humour that makes it compelling to read. 🍏

Sir, [...] there are a great many ingredients must go to the making me happy in a husband. First ... our humours must agree; and to do that he must have that kind of breeding that I have had and used that kind of company. That is, he must not be so much a country gentleman as to understand nothing but hawks and dogs, and be fonder of either than his wife; nor of the next sort of them whose aim reaches no further than to be Justice of Peace and once in his life High Sheriff, who reads no book but statutes and studies nothing but how to make a speech interlaced with Latin, that may amaze his poor disagreeing neighbours and fright them, rather than persuade them into quietness. He must not be a thing that began the world in a free school, was sent from thence to the university, and is at his farthest when he reaches the Inns of Court; has no acquaintance but those of his form in these places, speaks the French he has picked out of old laws, and admires nothing but the stories he has heard of the revels that were kept there before his time. He must not be a town gallant neither, that lives in a tavern and an ordinary that cannot imagine how an hour should be spent without company, unless it be in sleeping; that makes court to all the women he sees, thinks they believe him, laughs and is laughed at equally. Nor a travelled Monsieur whose head is all feather inside and outside, that can talk of nothing but dances and duels ... He must not be a fool of no sort, nor peevish, nor ill-natured, nor proud, nor covetous; and to all this must be added, that he must love me and I him, as much as we are capable of loving. Without all this his fortune, though never so great, would not satisfy me; and with it a very moderate one would keep me from repenting my disposal. [...] I am yours.

WILLIAM TEMPLE

Tuesda

my dearest life, I h[...]
morning & all the re[...]
writ ~~[crossed out]~~ every nigh[...]
have not come as th[...]
doe to take them in
w[hi]ch is the only time
them, the reason I[...]
but I wonder they ha[...]
you word, dd life, [...]
y[r] selfe, & the tean[...]
you is a double dea[...]
[...]d take take c[...]

'Get to me, if possible, before I die ... All my fear is I shall never see you'

Sir John Fenwick was an army officer and Jacobite conspirator. A strong partisan of King James II, he was briefly imprisoned in 1689 for plotting against King William III, who had ascended the throne in 1688 following the Protestant coup that became known as 'The Glorious Revolution'. In May 1691, Fenwick publicly mocked Queen Mary in St James's Park, an imprudent act that William would not forget. On his release from prison, Fenwick had continued his plotting and in February 1696 his plans for an armed insurrection were discovered, forcing him into hiding. In June of the same year, while attempting to flee to France, Fenwick was arrested. However, the government was unable to produce enough evidence to place him on trial for treason and so it was decided to proceed against him by Bill of Attainder. Fenwick therefore became the last Englishman to be tried for treason and condemned to death by Parliament. His devoted wife Mary tirelessly campaigned to save his life and a number of peers also protested against Fenwick's condemnation; but the king proved inexorable and gave his ascent to the bill on 11 January 1697. Fenwick sent this letter to Mary from Newgate Prison, shortly before his execution on Tower Hill on 28 January 1697. 🍒

Tuesday night

*My dearest life, I have yours [letter] of this morning and all the rest, and have
written every night, but they have not come as they used to do to take them
in the morning, which is the only time I can give them. The reason I know not,
but I wonder they have not sent you word. D[earest] d[earest] life, you will
kill yourself, and the fear I have for you is a double death to me. For God's sake
take care of yourself and destroy not your health. I know it is to no purpose, for
nothing but my blood will satisfy this man [i.e. the King]. Get to me if possible
before I die, sure he will not be so barbarous to deny that. I fear your petition
to the House will do no good but you have better advice than I can give. Pray
God give you success in it and that we may yet have a happy meeting. I burned
those letters I wrote for I dare not keep them, since I could not send them least
I should be searched, and there is an officer in the next room with soldiers with
him and a guard under the window who makes such a noise that I can get no*

Arrest of Sir John Fenwick

sleep and those in the next room perpetually smoking tobacco that it stinks into this room, that they had as good be in it, but I have none but Ashby in the room with me. [...] I expect every moment to have notice of the dead warrant, and then I suppose I shall be used with all barbarity. All my fear is I shall never see you, and that will make me distracted. If I must die, I should be glad you could get the favour I might be beheaded and not die the other shameful death. I shall want a flannel waist-coat, for these I have is a shame to have me stripped in before all the people, nor have I a whole shirt, these are all rags, one will serve me for that day, and I should have a nightcap of white satin with a Holland one under it turned upon it. I mention these things, but alas at the same time I know you have no money, and how you do to live God knows. It were as well for us both they took my life, for if he keeps me alive, he will seize of all we have, and then we should both starve. Pray God bless my dear Love, and bring you to my arms.

Pages 1, 3 and 4 of letter from Sir John Fenwick
to his wife, Mary, January 1697

with me, I think it not best to complain of it
any 10: Mungo — can get no rest for them, Jo
perhaps he may, wch will be best so certainly
such usage was never to a gentleman before
nor souldiers ever put in a county goale wch
is contrary to Law, the shirriffs rush are all
removed but Ashby, how long he may stay I
know not, I expect every moment to have
notice of the dead warrant, & then I suppose
I shall be used with all barbarity, all my
feare is I shall never see you, & that will make
me distracted, it I must dye I should be glad
you could get the favour I might be beheaded

3

& not dye the other shamefull death, I shall
want a flanell wastecoate for that I have is a
shame to have me wiped in before all the
people now have I a whole shirt, these are all
rags, one will serve me for that day, & I should
have a night capp of white satin with a holland
one under it turned upon it, I mention these things
but alass at the same time I know you have
no money & how you doe to live god knows.
It were well for us both they took my life
for if he keeps me alive he will seaze of all we
have & then we shall both starve, pray god
save my deare Love, & bring you to my armes

4

67

n as you could...

ld gett the better of your inclinat

often as you rememberd there was

if you continue to treat me as you

made uneasy by me long. tis impos

I have suffer'd since I saw you lo,

us'd have bore the Rack, much bet

g, killing words of yours. some

lov'd to die without seeing yo

resolves to your misfortune &

g. for there is something in hu

prompts one so to find relief i

give way to it. and beg you'd

kindly to me, for I am sure you

one to suffer what I have . on coul

reason I write to you, is because

should I see you. for when

you are angry, and there is some tha

wful, that it strikes me dumb. oh tha

so much regard for me left that th

touch your soul, with pitty. I Joy or

'I could have bore the rack much better than those killing, killing words of yours'

Jonathan Swift's tortured, triangular relationship with 'Stella' (Esther Johnson) and 'Vanessa' (Esther Van Homrigh) was the object of much speculation during his lifetime, and still attracts conjecture today. Born in Dublin in 1667, the author of *Gulliver's Travels* moved to England in 1689 and became secretary to government official Sir William Temple. It was in Temple's household that Swift met his life-companion, Stella, who in 1701 moved to Dublin with her chaperone, Rebecca Dingley, to take up residence near to St Patrick's Cathedral, where Swift had obtained the prebend. It was during a visit to London in 1710 that Swift met Vanessa, the daughter of a Dutch merchant and twenty-one years his junior. They struck up a correspondence and Swift immortalised his feelings for her in his most famous work of narrative poetry, *Cadenus and Vanessa*. Like Stella before her, Vanessa followed Swift to Dublin and took up residence there, with the result that the two women unwittingly competed for his attention. In this letter, Vanessa bitterly protests at her perceived ill-treatment by Swift and pleads for another meeting. It is said that when Swift finally ended their turbulent affair in 1723, Vanessa died of shock. 🌰

Dublin, 1714

Well now I plainly see how great a regard you have for me. You bid me be easy, and you'd see me as often as you could. You had better said, as often as you could get the better of your inclinations, so much, or as often as you remembered there was such a one in the world. If you continue to treat me as you do, you will not be made uneasy by me long. 'Tis impossible to describe what I have suffered since I saw you last; I am sure I could have bore the rack much better than those killing, killing words of yours. Sometimes I have resolved to die without seeing you more; but those resolves, to your misfortune, did not last long. For there is something in human nature that prompts one so to find relief in this world, I must give way to it, and beg you'd see me and speak kindly to me; for I am sure you'd not condemn any one to suffer what I have done, could you but know it.

The reason I write to you is because I cannot tell you, should I see you; for when I begin to complain, then you are angry, and there is something in your look so awful, that it strikes me dumb. Oh that you may but have so much regard for me left, that this complaint may touch your soul with pity. I say as little as ever I can: did you but know what I thought, I'm sure it would move you. Forgive me, and believe I cannot help telling you this, and live.

Dublin 1714
22
42

Well now I plainly see how great a regard you have for me. you bid me be easy, and you'd see me as often as you could. you had better said as often as you could gett the better of your inclenations, so much. or as often as you rememb'red there was such a one in the world. if you continue to treat me as you do, you will not be made uneasy by me long. tis imposible to discribe what I have suffer'd since I saw you last, I am sure I could have bore the Rack much better then those killing, killing, words of yours. some times I have resolved to die without seeing you more, but those resolves to your misfortune did not last long. for there is some thing in humain nature that prompts one so to find releife in this world I must give way to it. and beg you'd see me and speak kindly to me, for I am sure you'd not condemn any one to suffer what I have don could you but know it, the reason I write to you, is because I cannot tell it you, should I see you. for when I begin to complain then you are angry, and there is some thing in your look so awful, that it strikes me dumb. oh that you may but have so much regard for me left, that this complaint may touch your soul with pitty. I joy as little as ever can Did you but know what I thought I am sure it would move you to... believe I cannot self telling you this live...

Victory Octr: 19: 1805
Noon Cadiz E.S.E. 16 Leagues

My Dearest beloved Emma the dear
friend of my bosom the Signal has
been made that the Enemys Combined
fleet are coming out of Port, We
have very little Wind so that I have
no hopes of seeing them before tomorrow
may the God of Battles crown my
Endeavours with success at all events
I will take care that my name shall ever
be most dear to you and Horatia both
of whom I love as much as my own
life, and as my last writing before the
battle will be to you so I hope in God that
I shall live to finish my letter after the

'... as my last writing before the battle will be to you so I hope in God that I shall live to finish my letter after the Battle'

Lady Emma Hamilton and Horatio Nelson's passionate and adulterous love affair began some time in 1798. It scandalised the same society that revered Nelson for his military prowess, and has fascinated people ever since. During Nelson's long absences at sea, the two lovers had to communicate by letter. Afraid of exposure in the press, however, Nelson was very careful in his language to Emma, addressing her as his 'dearest friend' and never acknowledging the paternity of their daughter Horatia. Nelson also destroyed Emma's letters to him and urged her to do the same with those he sent her, but Emma could not bear to do so and kept every one. Few documents in the British Library's collections are more evocative than this, Nelson's final letter to Emma, which was found unfinished on his desk after he was fatally wounded by a French

musket ball while on the deck of the *Victory* during the Battle of Trafalgar. When the letter was delivered to Lady Hamilton by Captain Hardy, she added an anguished note to the end: 'Oh miserable wretched Emma, oh glorious & happy Nelson.' 🕊

Victory Oct[ob]er 19th 1805 Noon, Cadiz ESE 16 Leagues

My Dearest beloved Emma the dear friend of my bosom, the signal has been made that the enemys combined fleet are coming out of port. We have very little wind so that I have no hopes of seeing them before tomorrow. May the God of Battles crown my endeavours with success, at all events I will take care that my name shall ever be most dear to you and Horatia, both of whom I love as much as my own life. And as my last writing before the battle will be to you, so I hope in God that I shall live to finish my letter after the Battle. May heaven bless you prays your Nelson & Bronte. Oct[ob]er 20 in the morning we were close to the mouth of the Straits but the wind had not come far enough to the westward to allow the combined fleets to weather the shoals off Trafalgar but they were counted as far as forty sail of ships of war, which I suppose to be 34 of the line and six frigates. A group of them was seen off the lighthouse of Cadiz this morning but it blows so very fresh & thick weather that I rather believe they will get into the harbour before night. May God almighty give us success over these fellows and enable us to get a peace.

This letter was found open on his desk and brought to Lady Hamilton by Cap[tai]n Hardy.

Oh miserable wretched Emma
Oh glorious & happy Nelson.

and enable us to get a Peace

This letter was found open on his desk & brought to Lady Hamilton by Cap.tn Hardy

oh miserable wretched Emma

oh glorious & happy Nelson

...lle of friends and pursuits
...t your side. if you knew
...anxiety with which I wat...
...cts, the joy with which
...recovery, and the eagerne...
...would promote your
...cured more readily and
...tion of the pain ov...
..., but so difficult to

...Yours most affectionately
Charles Dickens.

'The sudden and uncalled-for coldness with which you treated me ... both surprised and deeply hurt me'

In May 1835 Charles Dickens became engaged to Catherine Hogarth, daughter of Charles Hogarth, editor of the *Evening Chronicle*. They were married on 2 April 1836 at St Luke's Church, Chelsea, and in the same month Dickens published the highly successful *Pickwick Papers*. Over the next twenty years the novelist published some of his most famous books, including *Oliver Twist, Nicholas Nickleby, A Christmas Carol, David Copperfield, Bleak House* and *Little Dorrit*. Despite establishing himself as the most popular writer in Britain, Dickens was intensely unhappy on a personal level, and had grown increasingly restless and dissatisfied in his marriage to Catherine, who had borne him ten children. In July 1857 Dickens befriended Ellen Lawless Ternan, an eighteen-year-old actress, and the following year was estranged from Catherine in a blaze of publicity. This letter, written just three weeks into Dickens's engagement to Catherine, shows that even before their marriage he had doubts about their compatibility. Although not a love letter proper, it does illustrate the intensity of Dickens's feelings for his wife-to-be, which as he reminded her 'has led me to forget all my friends and pursuits to spend my days at your side'. Catherine carefully preserved the letters she had received from her husband, both before and after marriage, so 'that the world may know he loved me once'. 💕

My dear Catherine,

 It is with the greatest pain that I sit down before I go to bed tonight, to say one word which can bear the appearance of unkindness or reproach; but I owe a duty to myself as well as to you, and as I was wild enough to think that an engagement of even three weeks might pass without any such display as you have favoured me with twice already, I am more strongly induced to discharge it.

 The sudden and uncalled-for coldness with which you treated me just before I left last night, both surprised and deeply hurt me – surprised, because I could not have believed that such sullen and inflexible obstinancy could exist in the breast of any girl in whose heart love had found a place; and hurt me, because I feel for you far more than I have ever professed, and feel a slight from you more than I care to tell. My object in writing to you is this: If a hasty temper produces this strange behaviour, acknowledge it when I give you the opportunity – not once or twice, but again and again. If a feeling of you know not what – a capricious restlessness of you can't tell what, and a desire to tease, you don't know why, give rise to it – overcome it; it will never make you more amiable, I more fond or either of us, more happy. If three weeks or three months of my society has wearied you, do not trifle with me, using me like any other toy as suits your humour for the moment; but make the acknowledgement to me frankly at once – I shall not forget you lightly, but you will need no second warning. Depend upon it, whatever be the cause of your unkindness – whatever gives rise to these wayward fancies – that what you do not take the trouble to conceal from a Lover's eyes, will be frequently acted before those of a husband.

I know as well, as if I were by your side at this moment, that your present impulse on reading this letter is one of anger – pride perhaps, or to use a word more current with your sex – 'spirit'. My dear girl, I have not the most remote intention of awakening any such feeling, and I implore you, not to entertain it for an instant. I am very little your superior in years: in no other respect can I lay claim to the title, but I venture nevertheless to give you advice first, because I cannot turn coolly away and forget a slight from you as I might from any other girl to whom I was not warmly and deeply attached; and secondly, because if you really love me I would have you do justice to yourself, and show me that your love for me, like mine for you, is above the ordinary trickery, and frivolous absurdity which debases the name and renders it ludicrous.

I have written these few lines in haste, but not in anger. I am not angry, but I am hurt, for the second time. Possibly you may not understand the sense in which I use the word; if so, I hope you never may. If you knew the intensity of the feeling which has led me to forget all my friends and pursuits to spend my days at your side; if you knew but half the anxiety with which I watched your recent illness, the joy with which I hailed your recovery, and the eagerness with which I would promote your happiness, you could more readily understand the extent of the pain so easily inflicted, but so difficult to be forgotten.

Ever yours most affectionately Charles Dickens

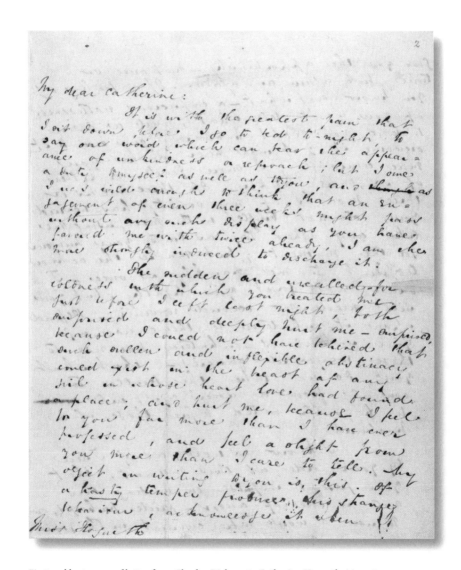

First and last pages of letter from Charles Dickens to Catherine Hogarth, May 1835

led me to forget all my friends and pursuits to
spend my days at your side. If you knew —
but half the anxiety with which I watched
your recent illness, the joy with which
I hailed your recovery, and the eagerness
with which I would promote your
happiness, you could more readily understand the extent of the pain so
easily inflicted, but so difficult to
be forgotten.

Ever Yours most affectionately

Charles Dickens.

Wednesday Morning

May 1835

Monsieur Hegum

No 32 Rue d'Iconville

Bruxelles

Belgique

'... truly I find it difficult to be cheerful so long as I think I shall never see you more'

In February 1842 Charlotte and Emily Brontë travelled to Brussels to study languages at the boarding school run by Professor Constantin Héger and his wife, Mme Héger. In return for their board and tuition, Charlotte taught English and Emily taught music. In October 1842 their studies were cut short by the death of their Aunt Elizabeth Branwell, who had cared for the Brontë household and children since the premature death of their mother. Charlotte returned alone to Brussels in January 1843, but her second stay proved less happy than her first. Desperately homesick and lonely as well as increasingly infatuated with Professor Héger, Charlotte decided to leave in January 1844. Following her return to England, Charlotte wrote to the Professor and incredibly four of her letters have survived, despite the fact that Professor Héger tore up three of them and threw all four away. Curiously, it is thanks to his wife – who retrieved them from the waste paper basket and sewed them back together – that we are privy to their content today. With the exception of one postscript, written in English, Charlotte wrote all four letters in French, the language that she associated with Héger. The letters are deeply poignant and reveal the extent of Charlotte's passionate feelings for the professor, her desire to see him, her despair at his silence and ultimately her resigned desolation and sense of rejection – emotions that she would later pour into *Jane Eyre* and *Villette*.

I must say one word to you in English – I wish I would write to you more cheerful letters, for when I read this over, I find it to be somewhat gloomy – but forgive me my dear master – do not be irritated at my sadness – according to the words of the Bible: 'Out of the fullness of the heart, the mouth speaketh' and truly I find it difficult to be cheerful so long as I think I shall never see you more. You will perceive by the defects in this letter that I am forgetting the French language – yet I read all the French books I can get, and learn daily a portion by heart – but I have never heard French spoken but once since I left Brussels – and then it sounded like music in my ears – every word was most precious to me because it reminded me of you – I love French for your sake with all my heart and soul.

Farewell my dear master – may God protect you with special care and crown you with peculiar blessings. CB

November 18th,
Haworth, Bradford, Yorkshire.

...nueil – je désiré

            Pois-je vous écrire encore au mois de M...
j'aurais voulu attendre toute une année – mais c'...
possible – c'est trop long.

                    C Brontë

...must say one word to you in English – I wish I...
write to you more cheerful letters, for when I read o...
...find it to be somewhat gloomy – but forgive me my
master – do not be irritated at my sadness – according to...
...f the Bible: "Out of the fullness of the heart, the mo...
...nd truly I find it difficult to be cheerful so long a...
...shall never see you more. You will perceive by t...
...n this letter that I am forgetting the French language...
...ad all the French books I can get, and learn dai...
...y heart – but I have never heard it French spoken b...
...ince I left Brussels – and then it sounded like m...
...ny ears – every word was most precious to me bee...
...minded me of you – I love French for your sak...
...ll my heart and soul.

            Farewell my dear Master – may God protect you ...
            care and crown you with peculiar blessings

...8th   CB.
    Haworth   Bradford   Yorkshire

XLIII

How do I love thee? Let me count the ways!—
I love thee to the depth & breadth & height
My soul can reach, when feeling out of sight
For the ends of Being and Ideal Grace.
I love thee to the level of everyday's
Most quiet need, by sun & candlelight—
I love thee freely, as men strive for Right;—
I love thee purely, as they turn from Praise:—
I love thee with the passion, put to use
In my old griefs; and ~~with~~ my childhood's faith
I love thee with the love I seemed to lose
With my lost ~~Saints~~ — I love thee with the breath,
Smiles, tears, of all my life!— and, if God choose,
I shall but love thee better after ~~an~~ death

ELIZABETH BARRETT BROWNING,
SONNET 43 FROM *SONNETS FROM THE PORTUGUESE*
C.1846

'How do I love thee?
Let me count the ways'

Elizabeth Barrett was already a famous poet when, in January 1845, Robert Browning wrote to her and declared, 'I love your verses with all my heart, dear Miss Barrett.' She replied, 'I thank you Mr Browning from the bottom of my heart', and so began a correspondence that led to their first meeting and eventually to their engagement, which was carefully concealed from Elizabeth's tyrannical father. On 12 September 1846 the couple married in secret at St Marylebone parish church, and a week later eloped to Italy and settled in Florence, where Elizabeth remained until her death in 1861. Perhaps it was the birth of their son in 1849 that prompted Elizabeth to show her husband the collection of sonnets that she had secretly written during their courtship. They movingly describe the gradual flowering of her love for Robert. This is the manuscript draft of perhaps the most famous of them all, 'How do I love thee?' The title, *Sonnets from the Portuguese*, is a reference to Robert's nickname for his wife, 'my little Portuguese', derived from her poem 'Catarina to Camoens'. Robert Browning outlived Elizabeth Barrett by twenty-eight years, but never remarried, declaring that his heart was buried in Florence. 🌰

How do I love thee? Let me count the ways.
I love thee to the depth and breadth and height
My soul can reach, when feeling out of sight
For the ends of Being and Ideal Grace.
I love thee to the level of everyday's
Most quiet need, by sun and candle-light.
I love thee freely, as men strive for Right;
I love thee purely, as they turn from Praise.
I love thee with the passion, put to use
In my old griefs, and with my childhood's faith.
I love thee with love I seemed to lose
With my lost saints – I love thee with the breath,
Smiles, tears, of all my life – and, if God choose,
I shall but love thee better after death.

I know this letter will
make you very angry
with me. but wait a little,
& dont say anything to
me which you are angry.
I promise not to sin any
more in the same way.

My ill health is caused
by the hopeless wretchedness
which weighs upon me.
I do not say this to pain
you, but because it is
the simple truth which

'I suppose no woman ever before wrote such a letter as this'

Mary Ann Evans, is best known for the seven novels she wrote under her pen name George Eliot, with *Middlemarch* often described as the greatest novel in the English language. Born in 1819 in Warwickshire, Eliot moved to London in 1851, where she found employment with the radical London publisher John Chapman as his editorial assistant on the *Westminster Review*. Through Chapman, Eliot met many of the leading writers and thinkers of the day, including the philosopher Herbert Spencer, one of the most famous European intellectuals of the age. Spencer described Eliot as 'the most admirable woman, mentally, I ever met', and they developed a close friendship, going to the theatre and opera and taking regular walks together. By 1852, Eliot was in love with Spencer but he found her lacking in beauty and could not reciprocate her feelings. This is her proud and painfully honest response to his rejection of her love. In 1854, Eliot shocked society by setting up home with the philosopher and critic George Henry Lewes, who already had a wife and children. Notwithstanding, Eliot considered herself to be married to Lewes, referring to him as her husband and signing herself Mary Ann Evans Lewes. She dedicated the manuscript of *The Mill on the Floss* 'To my beloved husband, George Henry Lewes'. In 1878 Lewes died and eighteen months later Eliot caused outrage again by marrying the banker John Walter Cross, some twenty years her junior. She fell ill seven months later and died on 22 December 1880 at the age of sixty-one. She was buried beside her beloved Lewes in London's Highgate Cemetery. 🐦

Broadstairs, Kent

I know this letter will make
you very angry with me,
but wait a little, and don't
say anything to me while
you are angry. I promise
not to sin any more in
the same way.
My ill health is
caused by the hopeless
wretchedness which
weighs upon me. I do not
say this to pain you, but
because it is the simple truth
which you must know in order
to understand why I am obliged to
seek relief.

I want to know if you can assure me that you will not forsake me,
and that you will always be with me as much as you can and share your
thoughts and feelings with me. If you become attached to some one else,
then I must die, but until then I could gather courage to work and make
life valuable, if only I had you near me. I do not ask you to sacrifice
anything – I would be very good and cheerful and never annoy you. But
I find it impossible to contemplate life under any other conditions. If I
had your assurance, I could trust that and live upon it. I have struggled
– indeed I have – to renounce everything and be entirely unselfish, but
I find myself utterly unequal to it. Those who have known me best have

always said, that if ever I loved any one thoroughly my whole life must turn upon that feeling, and I find they said truly. You curse the destiny which has made the feeling concentrate itself on you — but if you will only have patience with me you shall not curse it long. You will find that I can be satisfied with very little, if I am delivered from the dread of losing it.

I suppose no woman ever before wrote such a letter as this — but I am not ashamed of it, for I am conscious that in the light of reason and true refinement I am worthy of your respect and tenderness, whatever gross men or vulgar-minded women might think of me.

Friday

16. CHEYNE WALK
FRANGAS NON FLECTAS
CHELSEA

Funny sweet Janey

A bloke is coming
here tomorrow with
a frame, So I think I
had better take the
opportunity of sending
you that chalk drawing
as said bloke can hang
it up. If he should
happen not to come
tomorrow, then I suppose
he will on Monday, &
I will send it then.

Dear Janey, I suppose
this has come into my
head because I feel

'You are the noblest and dearest thing that the world has had to show me'

The English artist and poet, Dante Gabriel Rossetti, first met legendary Pre-Raphaelite muse Jane Morris (née Burden) in 1857, when he spotted her at a performance of the Drury Lane Theatre Company in Oxford. Captivated by her striking appearance, Rossetti asked Jane to model for him, thus beginning one of the most famous and enduring artist-model relationships, which inspired some of Rossetti's best paintings, such as *The Day Dream*. Rossetti and Jane were attracted to each other but he was already engaged to Lizzie Siddal, muse for John Everett Millais's *Ophelia*. In 1859 Jane married the artist and designer William Morris, although she would later confess that she never loved him. Following the death of a child in 1862, Lizzie committed suicide, plunging Rossetti into a deep depression. He and Jane gradually gravitated towards each other, embarking on an affair at some point in the late 1860s. They secretly exchanged letters whenever Jane was out of London; this one, sent by Rossetti to Jane in early 1870, reveals the extent to which she had become his obsession and the centre of his emotional life. Rossetti suffered a number of breakdowns in the 1870s and, although Jane continued to model for him, she broke off their romantic relationship in 1878 when she became aware of his dependency on alcohol and chloral hydrate, a drug taken for insomnia. On 11 December 1881, Rossetti suffered a mild stroke. He never fully recovered and died on Easter Sunday the following year, surrounded by family and close friends. Jane lived on at Kelmscott Manor until 1914 when she died aged seventy-five. 💕

16 Cheyne Walk, Chelsea
Friday

Funny sweet Janey,
A bloke is coming here tomorrow with a frame, so I think I had better
take the opportunity of sending you that chalk drawing as said bloke can
hang it up. If he should happen not to come tomorrow, then I suppose he
will on Monday, and I will send it then.

Dear Janey, I suppose this has come into my head because I feel so
badly the want of speaking to you. No one else seems alive at all to me
now, and places that are empty of you are empty of all life. And it is

so seldom that the dead
hours breathe a little and
yield your dear voice to
me again. I seem to hear
it while I write, and to
see your eyes speaking
as clearly as your voice;
and so I would write to
you for ever if it were not
too bad to keep reminding
you of my troubles, who
have so many of your
own. It is dreadful to me
to think constantly of a
sudden [sic] while my
mind longs for you, that
perhaps at that moment

you are suffering so much as to shut out even the possibility of pleasure if life had it ready for you in every shape. I always reproach myself with the comfort I feel despite all in the thought of you, when that thought never fails to present me also with the recollection of your pain and suffering. But more than all for me, dear Janey, is the fact that you exist, that I can yet look forward to seeing you and speaking to you again, and know for certain that at that moment I shall forget all my own troubles nor even to be able to remember yours. You are the

noblest and dearest thing that the world has had to show me; and if no lesser loss than the loss of you could have brought me so much bitterness, I would still rather have had to endure than have missed the fullness of wonder and worship which nothing else could have made known to me.

When I began this I meant to try and be cheerful, and just see what vague and dismal follies I have been inflicting on you – I hope to look in tomorrow evening and see how you are, even if I only stay half an hour.

Your most affectionate
Gabriel

1884.

Another year of joy & grief,
   Another year of hope & fear:
O Mother, is life long or brief?
   We hasten while we linger here.

But since we linger, love me still
   And bless me still, O Mother mine,
While hand in hand we scale life's hill
   You Guide, & I your Valentine.

'The Queen of Hearts'

Christina Rossetti, one of the most important female poets of the Victorian period, is perhaps best remembered today for her beautiful Christmas carol, 'In the Bleak Midwinter'. Born in London in 1830, Christina was a precocious child and shared the artistic and intellectual interests of her brothers, the Pre-Raphaelite artist Dante Gabriel and the writer and critic William Michael. Her engagement to the painter James Collinson, who, like her brothers, was a member of the Pre-Raphaelite group of artists, poets and critics, was broken off with much anguish when he joined the Roman Catholic Church; Christina remained all her life a devout High Anglican. Ill health meant that she led a quiet and confined existence, living with her mother to whom she remained steadfastly loyal. This is one of eleven charming short poems that Christina wrote for her mother as 'Valentines' between 1876 and 1886. Each one is inscribed on the reverse 'The Queen of Hearts'. On a separate sheet a pencil note in the poet's hand explains: 'These Valentines had their origins from my dearest Mother's remarking that she had never received one. I, her CGR, ever after supplied one on the day; and (so far as I recollect) it was a surprise every time, she having forgotten all about it in the interim.'

Dear Bosie,

After long and fruitless waiting I have determined to write to you myself, as much for your sake as for mine, as I would not like to think that I had passed through two long years of imprisonment without ever having received a single line from you, or any news or message even, except such as gave me pain.

Our ill-fated and most lamentable friendship has ended in ruin and public infamy for me, yet the memory of our ancient affection is often with me, and the thought that loathing, bitterness and contempt should for ever take that place in my heart once held by love is very sad to me: and you yourself will, I think, feel in your heart that to write to me as I lie in the loneliness of prison-life is better than to publish my letters without my permission or to dedicate poems to me unasked, though the world will know nothing of whatever words of grief or passion, of remorse or indifference you may choose to send as your answer or your appeal.

I have no doubt that in this letter in which I have to write of your life and of mine, of the past and of the future, of sweet things changed to bitterness and of bitter things that may be turned into joy, there will be much that will wound your vanity to the quick. If it prove so, read the letter over and over again till it kills your vanity. If you find in it something of which you feel that you are unjustly accused, remember that one should be thankful that there is any fault of which one can be unjustly accused. If there be in it one single passage that brings tears to your eyes, weep as we weep in prison where the day no less than the night is set apart for tears. It is the only thing that can save you. If you go complaining to your mother, as you did with reference to the scorn of you I displayed in my letter to Robbie, so that she may flatter and soothe you back into self-complacency or conceit, you will be completely lost. If you find one false excuse for yourself, you will soon find a hundred, and be just what you were before. Do you still say, as you said to Robbie in your answer, that I "attribute unworthy motives" to you? Ah! you had no motives in life. You had appetites merely. A motive is an intellectual aim. That you were "very young" when our friendship began? Your defect was not that you knew so little about life, but that you knew so much. The morning dawn of boyhood with its delicate bloom, its clear pure light, its joy of innocence and expectation you had left far behind. With very swift and running feet you had passed from Romance to

'After long and fruitless waiting I have determined to write to you myself, as much for your sake as for mine'

In 1895, the same year in which Oscar Wilde reached the height of his fame and success, with *An Ideal Husband* and *The Importance of Being Earnest* being performed on the stage in London, the writer was sentenced to two years' hard labour for homosexual offences. In 1884 Wilde had married Constance Lloyd, who bore him two sons, but some time in 1891 he met and fell in love with Lord Alfred Douglas, known to friends and family as Bosie. Their affair had disastrous consequences for Wilde, who, after being publicly insulted by Lord Alfred's father, the ninth Marquess of Queensberry, sued for criminal libel, triggering a chain of events that led to his imprisonment and public disgrace. Shown here are the first and last pages of 'De Profundis', the 50,000-word letter that Wilde wrote to Douglas from Reading Gaol between December 1896 and March 1897. As well as charting Wilde's spiritual growth through the physical and emotional hardships of his imprisonment, the letter is a bitter indictment of the man who he felt had helped to destroy his life and reputation. It is also one of the great love letters of history, in which Wilde acknowledges that even though 'our ill-fated and most lamentable friendship has ended in ruin and public infamy for me, yet the memory of our ancient affection is often with me, and the thought that loathing, bitterness and contempt should for ever take that place in my heart held by love is very sad to me'. 🍏

H.M. Prison, Reading

Dear Bosie,

After a long and fruitless waiting I have determined to write to you myself, as much for your sake as for mine, as I would not like to think that I had passed through two long years of imprisonment without ever having received a single line from you, or any news or message even, except such as gave me pain.

Our ill-fated and most lamentable friendship has ended in ruin and public infamy for me, yet the memory of our ancient affection is often with me, and the thought that loathing, bitterness and contempt should for ever take that place in my heart once held by love is very sad to me: and you yourself will, I think, feel in your heart that to write to me as I lie in the loneliness of prison-life is better than to publish my letters without my permission or to dedicate poems to me unasked, though the world will know nothing of whatever words of grief or passion, of remorse or indifference you may choose to send as your answer or your appeal.

I have no doubt that in this letter in which I have to write of your life and mine, of the past and of the future, of sweet things changed to bitterness and of bitter things that may be turned into joy, there will be much that will wound your vanity to the quick. If it prove so, read the letter over and over again till it kills your vanity. If you find in it something of which you feel that you are unjustly accused, remember that one should be thankful that there is any fault of which one can be unjustly accused. If there be in it one single passage that brings tears to your eyes, weep as we weep in prison where the day no less than the night is set apart for tears. It is the only thing that can save you. [...] Your defect was not that you knew so little about life, but that you knew so much. The morning dawn of boyhood with its delicate bloom, its clear pure light, its joy of innocence and expectation you had left far behind. With very swift and running feet you had passed from Romance to Realism. The gutter and the things that live in it had begun to fascinate you. That was the origin of the trouble in which you sought my aid. [...]

At the end of a month when the June roses are in all their wanton opulence, I will, if I feel able, arrange through Robbie to meet you in some quiet foreign town like Bruges, whose grey houses and green canals and cool still ways had a charm for me, years ago. [...] I hope that our meeting will be what a meeting between you and me should be, after everything that has occurred. In old days there was always a wide chasm between us, the chasm of achieved art and acquired culture: there is a still wider chasm between us now, the chasm of Sorrow: but to Humility there is nothing that is impossible, and to Love all things are easy. [...]

What lies before me is my past. I have got to make myself look on that with different eyes, to make the world look on it with different eyes, to make God look on it with different eyes, this I cannot do by ignoring it, or slighting it, or praising it, or denying it. It is only to be done by fully accepting it as an inevitable part of the evolution of my life and character: by bowing my head to everything that I have suffered. How far I am away from the true temper of soul, this letter in its changing, uncertain moods, its scorn & bitterness, its aspirations & its failure to realise those aspirations, shows you quite clearly. But do not forget in what a terrible school I am sitting at my task. And incomplete, imperfect, as I am, yet from me you may have still much to gain. You came to me to learn the Pleasure of Life and the Pleasure of Art. Perhaps I am chosen to teach you something much more wonderful, the meaning of Sorrow, and its beauty,

Your affectionate friend, Oscar Wilde

... my name, once so musical in the mouth of fame, will have to be abandoned by me, in turn. How narrow, and mean, and inadequate to its burdens this century of ours! It can give to Success its palace of porphyry, but for Sorrow and Shame it does not keep even a wattled house in which they may dwell: all it can do for me is to bid me change my name into some other name where mediaevalism would have given me the cowl of the monk or the face-cloth of the leper behind which I might be at peace..... I hope that our meeting will be what a meeting between you and me should be, after all that has occurred. In old days there was always a wide chasm between us, the chasm of achieved Art and acquired culture: there is a still wider chasm between us now, the chasm of Sorrow: but to Humility there is nothing that is impossible, and to Love all things are easy.

As regards your letter to me in answer to this, it may be as long or as short as you choose. Address the envelope to 'the Governor. H. M. Prison. Reading': inside, in another, and an open envelope, place your own letter to me: if your paper is very thin do not write on both sides, as it makes it hard for others to read. I have written to you with perfect freedom. You can write to me with the same. What I must know from you is why you have never made any attempt to write to me, since the August of the year before last, more especially after, in the May of last year, ten months ago now, you knew, and admitted to others that you knew, that you had made me suffer, and how I realise it. I waited month after month to hear from you. Even if I had not been waiting but had shut the door against you, you should have remembered that no one can possibly shut the door against Love for ever. The unjust judge in the Gospels rises up at length to give a just decision because Justice came knocking daily at his door, at night-time. At the friend, in short hearted, there is no real friendship yields at length to his friend because of his importunity. In any words which faces an entrance there is no prison Love cannot. If you did not understand that, you did not understand anything about Love at all. Then, let me know all about your article on me for the Mercure de France. I know something of it. You had better quote from it. It is set up in type. Also, let me know the exact terms of your Dedication of your poems. If it is in prose, quote the prose: if in verse, quote the verse: write to me with full frankness about yourself: about your life: your friends: your occupations: your books. Tell me about your volume and its reception. Whatever you have to say for yourself, say it without fear. Don't write anything you don't mean. If there is anything in your letter, if it is false or counterfeit I shall detect it by the ring at once. It is not for nothing or to no purpose, that in my life-long cult of literature I have made myself

'master of sound and syllable, no less
than midas of his coinage.'

Remember, too, that I have yet to know you. Perhaps we have yet to know each other.

For yourself, I have but this last thing to say. Do not be afraid of the past. If people tell you that it is irrevocable, do not believe them. The past, the present and the future are but one moment in the sight of God, in whose sight we should try to live. Time and space, succession and extension, are merely accidental conditions of Thought. The Imagination can transcend them, and move in a free sphere of ideal existences. Things, also, are in their essence what we choose to make them. A thing is, according to the mode in which one looks at it. 'Where others,' says Blake, 'see but the Dawn coming over the hill, I see the sons of God shouting for joy.' What seemed to the world and to myself my future I lost irretrievably when I let myself be taunted into taking the action against your father: had I done so, lost it really long before that. What lies before me is my past. I have got to make myself look on that with different eyes, to make the world look on it with different eyes, to make God look on it with different eyes. This I cannot do by ignoring it, or slighting it, or praising it, or denying it. It is only to be done by fully accepting it as an inevitable part of the evolution of my life and character: by bowing my head to everything that I have suffered. How far I am away from the true temper of soul, this letter in its changing, uncertain moods, its scorn and bitterness, its aspirations and its failure to realise those aspirations, shows you quite clearly. But do not forget in what a terrible school I am sitting at my task. And incomplete, imperfect, as I am, yet from me you may still have much to gain. You came to me to learn the Pleasure of Life and the Pleasure of Art. Perhaps I am chosen to teach you something much more wonderful, the meaning of Sorrow, and its beauty.

your affectionate friend
Oscar Wilde

never less than that; only
this letter, for then you wi
want it; and just say so f
yourself sometimes

"I have a friend acros
I like him, but he love
And come to me on your ou
for I cannot do without you
True, you will be cons
my love; but let that assu
I shall never do anything
to you.

At any rate, once i
I feel blessed and made
having written myself dow
lover Gordon Bottomley

'More private than the unshaped wish at the centre of your heart'

The Yorkshire poet and playwright Gordon Bottomley (1874–1948) was incapacitated by crippling ill health for most of his life. He accepted his condition as a 'fine opportunity to live a life of passionate, intense meditation and contemplation – a life of the spirit concentrated upon the nature and processes of spiritual creation, as that is manifested in the arts which is man's most permanent achievement'. His interest in the arts found a natural outlet in correspondence, and his letters to many of the leading artists, writers, theatre directors and composers of the day are now stored in 120 volumes at the British Library. Bottomley's archive also contains some 500 letters that he wrote to the artist Emily Burton from 1895, during their early friendship and engagement, until their marriage in 1905. Bottomley had a masterful way with words and wrote with drama and passion, qualities that can also be found in this beautifully written letter from October 1899 in which he finally revealed

his feelings to Emily. The couple lived most of their married life in Silverdale, near Carnforth in Lancashire. When Emily died in 1947, Bottomley was lost without her selfless and devoted companionship and outlived her by less than a year. 🌑

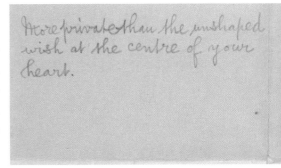

Well Knowe *October 17th, 1899*

Dear My Lady

I can bear no longer to simulate a friendship for you which is less than what I feel; ever since I have known you I have had a thing in my heart to say to you, and in April last I determined to say it some day.

For a long time I thought it was my duty to leave this thing unsaid; so I did my duty, and it made me cross and irritable and bad-tempered to everyone, and, I fear, unkind even to you.

O, how I hope that I am not estranging you even when I tell you that I love you wholly, that as long as I have known you, you have been to me 'half angel and half bird and all a wonder and a wild desire', that your influence alone can waken what is best in me, that if I had not been penniless and helpless and

dependent upon my parents I should long ago have asked you to marry me.

(That poem Green Coif is as much about you as if it had your name for its title, and is and always was as much addressed to you as this letter is.)

But at one time I thought you were likely to marry a Liverpool artist-friend, a man of a finer and rarer spirit than I am; a man who would give you the life-atmosphere you need; and I loved you well enough to know how far more excellent this was than anything I could give you.

However, I have since thought that if you love him my speaking cannot draw you away from him; and that if your heart turns to me more than to other men (as my heart turns to you and to no other woman) then my keeping silent will not make you love him.

But how uncouthly, nay, barbarically, I have shown my love for you.

Ah, you think me a better and an abler man than I am; my one good-deed has been to recognize and reverence a great-hearted crystal-souled woman until she has become my true inspiration; this letter is the best poem I shall ever write in all my life.

I love you; I do not know how to say anything else.

If you care for me in this way, you will tell me, won't you?

But if this is all a mistake, if you can be no more to me than the friend you have always been, I beseech you to be never less than that; only, burn this letter, for then you will not want it; and just say softly to yourself sometimes

   'I have a friend across the sea
   I like him, but he loves me'

And come to me on your own terms, for I cannot do without you.

True, you will be conscious of my love; but let that assure you I shall never do anything distasteful to you.

At any rate, once in eternity I feel blessed and made glorious, having written myself down your lover.

   Gordon Bottomley.

Well Knowe.   Oct. 17th. 1899

Dear My Lady,
        I can bear no longer to simula[te]
a friendship for you which is less [than]
than what I feel; ever since I
have known you I have had a thin[g]
in my heart to say to you, and in
April last I determined to say it
some day.
        For a long time I thought [it]
was my duty to leave this thing
unsaid; so I did my duty, and it
made me cross and irritable an[d]
bad-tempered to everyone, and, I
fear, unkind even to you.
        O, how I hope that I am not
estranging you when I tell you th[at]
I love you wholly, that as long a[s]
I have known you you have be[en]
to me "half angel and half bir[d]"
And all a wonder and a wild desi[re]
that your influence alone can wak[e]
what is best in me, that if I ha[d]
not been penniless and helpless an[d]
dependent upon my parents I sho[uld]
long ago have asked you to
marry me.

(That poem "Green Corn" is as much about you as if it had your name for its title, and is and always was as much addressed to you as this letter is.

But at one time I thought you were likely to marry a Liverpool artist-friend, a man of a finer and rarer spirit than I am — a man who would give you the life-atmosphere you need; and I loved you well enough to know how far more excellent this was than anything I could give you.

However, I have since thought that if you love him my speaking cannot draw you away from him; and that if your heart turns to me more than to other men (as my heart turns to you and to no other woman) then my keeping silent will not make you love him.

But how uncouthly, nay barbarically, I have shewn my love for you.

Ah, you think me a better and an abler man than I am; my one good deed has been to recognize and reverence a great-hearted crystal-souled woman until she has become my true inspiration; this letter is the best poem I shall ever write in all my life.

I love you; I do not know how to say anything else.

If you care for me in this way, you will tell me, won't you?

my heart goes knocking when I think
I don't understand — —
of it.

Little child, I will kiss you till I kill you.
Be gentle with me.

Goodnight

Rupert

Do not answer anything.
I like writing it
of fact briefly.

I write this becau
But answer privili
is a practical world

'I'm madly eager to see you again. My heart goes knocking when I think of it.'

In 2007 the British Library acquired a collection of eighty-two love letters written by the First World War poet Rupert Brooke to the English actress Cathleen Nesbitt. The previously unseen letters provide a fascinating insight into their two-year romance, which began when Brooke fell under Cathleen's spell while watching her performance as Perdita in *A Winter's Tale* at the Savoy Theatre in London. This letter, written in early 1913, shows how Brooke – once referred to by W.B.Yeats as 'the most handsome man in the country' – was captivated by Cathleen and worshipped 'her great beauty'. In another letter he wrote: 'Haven't you noticed your chin and neck are the most beautiful thing in the world? Haven't you heard about your hair? Has nobody told you about your eyes? Haven't you read in the papers that your lips are maddening?' Brooke bombarded her with marriage proposals and made frequent references to a life with 'lots of lovely children' away from the hustle and bustle of London. Brooke tragically died from blood poisoning on 23 April 1915, while on his way to fight in the fateful Gallipoli campaign. As if intuiting his approaching death, he wrote to Cathleen from 'off Gallipoli' on 18 March: 'Oh my dear, Life is a very good thing. Thank God I met you. Be happy and be good. You have been good to me. Goodbye, dearest child – Rupert.' 🍒

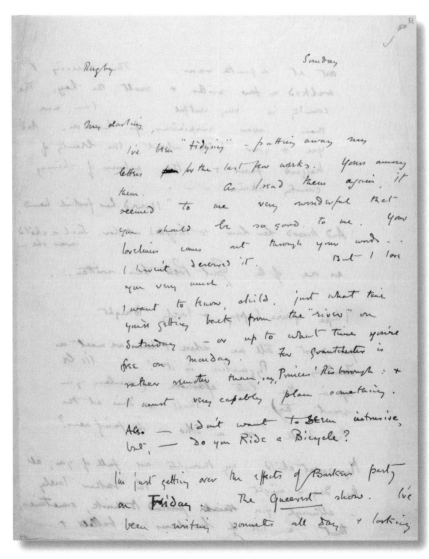

Pages 1 and 2 of letter from Rupert Brooke to Cathleen Nesbitt, 1913

out at a gentle rain. This evening I
walked a few miles + smelt the hay. The
country is very restful. I am more
than ever suspicious of London. And
you + your talk about the beauty of
haggard faces + the ugliness of shining
country skins — — —

"I bowed her foolish head,
And kissed her hair + laughed at her. Such a child
was she ..."

as one of the Great Poets has written.

I hope you're happy + lovely tonight.

You must tell me where + how we meet on
Tuesday. Pygmalion is it? I'll be
up in the late afternoon (unless you
want tea). Shall we dine at the
Pall Mall? or in Soho — it's fairly near? —

My sweet child, my thoughts are full of you, all
the day + night. I'm rather lonely
— although you pretend to think, sometimes,
that a life of luncheons + ballets +

Rugby   *Sunday*

My darling,

    I've been 'tidying' – putting away my letters for the last few weeks.
Yours among them. As I read them again, it seemed to me very wonderful that
you should be so good to me. Your loveliness comes out through your words …
I haven't deserved it. But I love you very much. […]

    I've been writing sonnets all day and looking out at a gentle rain. This
evening I walked a few miles and smelt the hay. The country is very restful. I am
more than ever suspicious of London. And you and your talk about the beauty of

haggard faces and the ugliness of shining
country skies …

    'I bowed her foolish head, And kissed
her hair and laughed at her. Such a child
was she …' as one of the Great Poets has
written.

    I hope you are happy and lovely tonight.
You must tell me where and how we meet
on Tuesday. Pygmalion is it? I'll be up in the
late afternoon (when you want tea). Shall
we dine at the Pall Mall? Or in Soho – it's
fairly near?

    My sweet child, my thoughts are full
of you, all the day and night. I'm rather
lonely – although you pretend to think,
sometimes, that a life of luncheon and

ballets and suppers 'is all the human heart
requires'. I'm a fool: but I do know that one
needs other things. One thing I need – only one
of many, but a strong one – oh! I know it is a
great feebleness – is to worship. There aren't,
these days, many things we can worship.
I've found one: your great beauty. Thank God
I found it.

Oh, but – it's the terrifyingly glad part of
it – you're not only goddess; you're also child.
Both at once: – what colour is shot silk? –
That's what sends my blood beating to my head
till I'm dizzy.

Cathleen, my darling, it is very wonderful
when we're together. I wish to God you were
coming in through the door now: and that I
could hold your hands. There's beauty when we're together. I understand –
in a way I understand you completely: because I love you so.

I'm madly eager to see you again. My heart goes knocking when I think of it.
I don't understand ………

Little child, I will kiss you till I kill you. Be gentle with me.

Goodnight

Rupert

Do not answer lengthily. I write this because I like writing it. But answer points
of fact briefly. It's a practical world.

My darling Eva

I don't quite know why I am writing this – but one never knows one's luck and one can't say that one is certain to come back from an enterprise such as the one I hope to take part in ~~to~~ on Sunday morning – And so if we are to part company, for a bit, I want to tell you

'I want to tell you … how blissfully happy I have been with you my Sweet Red Rose'

Sir Roger Keyes, one of the twentieth century's most important naval figures, enjoyed a distinguished career that spanned two world wars. Born in India on 4 October 1872, he joined the Royal Navy as a cadet in 1885 and when he married Eva Salvin on 10 April 1906 he had already reached the rank of Captain. Keyes served as Commander in charge of submarines from 1910 to 1914 and it was during this period, with England at war with Germany, that he wrote this letter to his wife and sealed it in an envelope marked 'Eva, Please do not open this until you hear of my death'. For obvious reasons, Keyes did not explain to his wife the nature of the enterprise that he was about to take part in, but history reveals that Keyes was preparing to join the Cuxhaven Raid, a particularly dangerous British ship-based air-raid on the Zeppelin sheds at Cuxhaven, originally scheduled for 11 December 1914 but then postponed until 25 December. Keyes survived the raid, returned home and the letter remained unopened. Years later, having retired from the navy as Admiral of the Fleet and been elevated to the peerage as Baron Keyes of Zeebrugge and Dover in 1943, he was sent on a goodwill mission to America, Canada, Australia and New Zealand. It was only then, in June 1944, that as a note added to the envelope by Eva Keyes reveals, the letter was 'opened at R[oger's] request before going round world'. 🦋

HMS Maidstone 10th December 1914

My darling Eva,

I don't quite know why I am writing this – but one never knows one's luck and one can't say that one is certain to come back from an enterprise such as the one I hope to take part in on Sunday morning – and so if we are to part company, for a bit, I want to tell you before I go on my long journey how blissfully happy I have been with you my Sweet Red Rose. It is hard to believe that this will be the end of our partnership, and I will go in the hope that we will unite again in another world. I know mine is the easier part, but I know you will show a gallant part and live for those sweet babas – and the other to come. I would like you to ask Reggie Tyrwhitt to be godfather – particularly mentioning the day this request was written. I know you will always be sweet and kind to my mother and sister – as you have ever been. Much as I would like to live to share many more happy years with you darling, it is proper and right to be ready to die at such a time and I know you will give me credit for going out very confidently and buoyantly to meet my fate. May the God I believe in be with you and the babas always. With all my love and all my thanks for your dear love.

I am your very devoted Roger.

10/12/14 · Roger

Eva.

Please do not open this until you hear of my death. Opened at R: request before going round world June 1944

EK

The Mill House,
Tidmarsh,
Pangbourne.

Sunday morning 8 May. 1921.

Dearest. precisely nine o'ch. But move vaguely

I have no idea what you are doing at this moment what you look at, whether you glide in the train over alps, or shiver on an Italian station wrapt in your great cloak — You know what the sitting room looks like, and the view from this window — Your visions I can't even guess! #15 monday morning now

& I am writing sadly. So forgive the tinge of melancholy, if it creeps into these pages.

I will tell you everything which has happened since you floated away with your hats, & boxes in the train from Euston Square — I dashed off almost at once in a taxi to the Grosvenor Gallery with a nameless picture just in time, as Roger had started hanging. I took the tulips, I didn't much like it, But I hadn't anything else small enough. ... Somehow I feel rather despondent about the painting. It never seems anything like as good as what I conceive inside. Everything is a failure when its finished. They start off so full of hope — I hope Giotto, & the Florentine may brisk up my powers. lunch with Ralph at 41, G.S. and then a five o'ch train to Pangbourne. We found Barbara & Nick busy gardening. & very happy.

'… you are <u>too</u> good. So charming that I'd like to serve you all my life'

The artist Dora Carrington was a prolific writer and between 1915 and 1932 she penned hundreds of vivid letters that paint a fascinating portrait of her unconventional relationships and home life. Carrington first met Lytton Strachey, author of *Eminent Victorians* and member of the Bloomsbury Group in 1915 and, although he was openly homosexual and thirteen years her senior, she fell deeply in love with him. They set up home together at Mill House, Tidmarsh, in Berkshire, and Carrington tended to Strachey's every need throughout their intense but mainly platonic relationship, which lasted until his death in 1932. Carrington sometimes struggled with Strachey's lack of interest in what he referred to as 'the physical' and explored other romantic relationships, while remaining utterly devoted to him. In this deeply affectionate letter to Strachey, Carrington confides that Ralph Partridge, who had fallen in love with her in 1918, had become increasingly anxious to marry her. She reluctantly agreed to become his wife because Strachey also adored Ralph and she worried that turning him down would result in the break-up of their menage à trois. Almost immediately, however, Carrington began an affair with Gerald Brenan, one of Ralph's best friends. In 1931 Strachey fell ill with stomach cancer and died on 21 January 1932. Carrington confided in Virginia Woolf, 'There is nothing left for me to do. I did everything for Lytton. But I've failed in everything else.' Unable to contemplate life without her 'bearded poet', she shot herself seven weeks after his death. 🐦

The Mill House, Tidmarsh, Pangbourne
<u>*Sunday*</u>*. Precisely 9 o'ck. But more vaguely morning. 8 May 1921*

Dearest
I have no idea what <u>you</u> are doing, what you look at, whether you glide
in the train over alps at this moment, or shiver in an Italian station room
wrapt [sic] in your great cloak. You know what the sitting room looks
like, and the view from this window: <u>your</u> visions I can't even guess!
It's Monday morning now and I am writing sadly. So forgive the tinge
of melancholy, if it creeps into these pages. I will tell <u>you</u> everything
which has happened since you floated away with your hats, & boxes
in the rain from Gordon Square – I dashed off almost at once in a
taxi to the Grosvenor Gallery with a nameless picture just in time, as
Roger had started hanging. I took the tulips, I didn't much like it. But I
hadn't anything else small enough … somehow I feel rather despondent
about the painting. It never seems to be anything like as good as what
I conceive inside. Everything is a failure when it's finished. They start
off so full of life – I hope Giotto and the Florentines may brisk up my
powers. Lunch with Ralph at 41 G.S. and then a five o'clock train to
Pangbourne. […]
Ralph is now upset also. And heaps coal of fire on my head! Then
he's angry today because I stayed behind to finish my greyhound. He
never sees that it's very tedious for me to be in London all the week if
I've no painting to do. And he can't understand that sometimes one can
work better in the country than in London. But I won't impose lovers'
quarrels on you – Only it is a little difficult. He has had a mania for
getting married lately … He thinks it will be easier to go to Italy à deux
and make things easier living at G.S. afterwards. There is something

in it of course. But if we are going to be at loggerheads when I want to live here alone, perhaps it's better to not be married! Au fond the real difficulty is he likes me always to be with him, and sometimes I prefer this life here. ~~ This morning he went off in a rage and Italy seemed to vanish with him. ~~ You know dear he only first told me this weekend that you are going to pay for our tickets. I cannot thank you, you are <u>too</u> good. So charming that I'd like to serve you all my life. Thank you very much indeed. 'Too kind, too kind' she murmured xxx and forty hugs for Blue Beard.

Dear, there is so much to say to you, yet I can write nothing … I want to tell you that I miss you very much yet it sounds so bleak without the exactitude of feeling which I'd like to express. I hope you will be very happy in Florence … And keep well. Please, when there is time send me jottings, about the people at the villa, the view from the windows and the pictures you see in the galleries. We <u>must</u> come! And I'll give up everything to humour that Barbarian if only to bask under Italy's sun. But he <u>is</u> a savage you know and I am a stoopid little Mopsa I suppose and you, the wisest, best loveliest bearded poet alive. X X X X

My sweetest, my most dear darling Maeve

Today you will be going into
the Nursing Home. I hope that
everything will work smoothly & that
everyone will be gentle to you, my
dear little wife. I have had
no definite news as to whether I
can come or not but I will do
my utmost. How wonderful
it was to be able to talk to
you last night, dear Maeve.
As I told you, I was speaking
from that family I told you
about. They gave me high tea
when I dropped in about 6 pm
and I told them about

'You are in my heart, darling. I am loving you more than I have ever done before'

Mervyn Peake, best known today as the author of *Gormenghast*, was a uniquely talented artist and writer. Although he failed to shine academically, his creative gifts were apparent at an early age and nurtured by his teacher Eric Drake. After leaving school, Peake enrolled at Croydon School of Art and then briefly attended the Royal Academy Schools. In 1935 he was offered a teaching position at Westminster School of Art and it was here that he met the artist Maeve Gilmore, who had enrolled in sculpture classes. They married on 1 December 1937 and had two sons, Sebastian and Fabian, and a daughter, Clare. The first two decades of family life were spent in London, on Sark, in Kent and Surrey; later, in her memoir, *A World Away*, Maeve would recall these years as idyllic and marvellously fulfilling. From the middle of the 1950s Parkinson's disease gradually prevented Peake from working and led to his premature death in 1968. His archive, acquired by the British Library in 2010, includes a collection of personal letters from Peake to his wife. These were often, as the one received by Maeve just before she was due to give birth demonstrates, charmingly illustrated by the uxorious Peake. 🍒

My sweetest, my most dear darling Maeve,

Today you will be going into the nursing home. I hope that everything will work smoothly and that everyone will be gentle to you, my dear little wife. I have had no definite news as to whether I can come or not but I will do my utmost. How wonderful it was to be able to talk to you last night, dear Maeve. As I told you, I was speaking from that family I told you about. They gave me high tea when I dropped in about 6pm and I told them about you. I want to tell everyone about you – about your beauty – your sweetness, your paintings.

Are you feeling very imminent, Maeve. Do you feel worried or can you detatch yourself at all. Oh darling, how I love you. How I love you.

Perhaps when this reaches you the little baby will be borne.

Oh Maeve. You are in my heart, darling. I am loving you more than I have ever done before. Bless you – oh my sweetheart, bless you. Bless you.

I am longing for your release. I am longing for news, and to be with you.

Maevie. I am in love. Deeply. Un-endingly, for ever and ever.

Your Mervyn

THE DORCHESTER HOTEL
LONDON
TELEPHONE: MAYFAIR 8888

Monday. 1. 11. 48
11. 30 pm

My darling Joan,

It was a lovely letter from you
this morning: I keep re-reading it to cheer myself
up. I read all your letters many times - they are
all I can have for another 7 days. You are
necessary to me not just for happiness or peace.
but for life itself - I cease to have any desires
or wishes or hopes that are not bound up with you

Perhaps if there is a letter from you in
the morning it will tell me what you think
about the Half Way Playhouse - I'm becoming
Schizophrenic about it. We said we'd take
a building anywhere, but this one is so far removed

'You are necessary to me not just for happiness of peace, but for life itself'

Gerry Raffles first met the visionary theatre director Joan Littlewood in the late 1930s when he joined Theatre Union, the amateur company established to create intelligent popular theatre for those to whom theatre was unfamiliar. Joan was married and eight years Gerry's senior but they fell deeply in love and became lifelong partners. Theatre Union was disbanded in 1942 but reformed after the war as the professional company Theatre Workshop, which initially operated as an itinerant creative ensemble, playing to predominantly working-class audiences in Britain, Scandinavia, Germany and Czechoslovakia. Gerry regularly travelled ahead of the company in order to secure work, and on this occasion he was in England eagerly anticipating Joan's return from Sweden, while searching for a base for the company and a place for Joan and himself to live. Keen to meet with the People's Entertainments Society, Gerry caught a lift to London with his brother Eric. Typically, Gerry didn't have anywhere to stay and so whiled away the night at Lyon's Corner House, before meeting up with Eric, who was staying at the Dorchester, for breakfast. In 1953, Theatre Workshop moved to the Theatre Royal in Stratford East, London, and over the next two decades won acclaim for productions such as *A Taste of Honey* (1958) and *Oh What a Lovely War* (1963). Gerry was Joan's rock; he was the organisational driving force behind Theatre Workshop and took care of their domestic life. When he died suddenly on holiday in 1975, Joan was grief-stricken. She left the theatre for good and moved to France to be near to his grave at Vienne, near Lyons. ❧

7 DAYS TO GO
London
Monday. 1.11.48
11.30pm

My darling Joan,
It was a lovely letter from you this morning: I keep re-reading it to
cheer myself up. I read all your letters many times – they are all I can
have for another 7 days. You are necessary to me not just for happiness
or peace, but for life itself – I cease to have any desires or wishes or hopes
that are not bound up with you.

Perhaps if there is a letter from you in the morning it will tell
me what you think about the Half Way Playhouse – I'm becoming
schizophrenic about it. We said that we'd take a building anywhere, but
this one is so far removed from any working class district as to make it
impossible to draw a working class audience. It is true that whatever
seating arrangements we made could be designed so as to be usable when
and if we eventually secure the other building. It has taken me nearly
one hour to write the little piece about the building. In contact with you
I am stimulated anew to critical enamoration and now I find myself
more and more accepting the inevitability and desirability of taking this
building, as far as it is from ideal. The task of launching it, however,
is immense. It is a small building, and the seating will have to be very
carefully planned to reach an economic figure. ...

Sweet love one week from now – if I can find somewhere for us to
live – I will be holding you in my arms and I hope the bed doesn't creak.
I wonder have I ever been satiated with you, and if so, what it felt like. I
feel like a camel who looks forward to the oasis 7 days ahead, but I never

had a chance to drink my fill first, that is what you are really like, a cool draught in a desert, a warm toddy on a mountain, a heady wine in love. Always life giving, always intoxicating, always invigorating. And for you my thirsts are infinite. You are the thirst quencher that can be drunk or swam in. I do both so that I drown in your lapping warmth. What a perfect death! And do I need you now!! If your mouths are as open for me as my thirsts are for you ....!

As I say goodnight I kiss your nipples and your breasts, your shoulders, neck, lips, your belly and your thighs and your seat of all pleasures. Oh to give my tongue a roving license.

Good night dear love, I hope you dream about

Your Gerry

RALPH RICHARDSON

26 JAN 70

Dearest Fernety,

Love

and many happy
returnes.

R.

'Dearest Ferrety'

Sir Ralph Richardson was one of the foremost stage and screen actors of his generation. He was born in 1902 in Cheltenham, Gloucestershire, where his father was art master at Cheltenham Ladies' College. He started his working life as an office boy for the Liverpool and Victoria Insurance Company in Brighton and then spent a short time at Brighton Art College, before deciding that he wanted to become an actor. On 18 September 1924 Richardson married the seventeen-year-old student-actress Muriel ('Kit') Hewitt. The following year the newlyweds joined the Birmingham Repertory Company, and Richardson made his first stage appearance in London for the Greek Play Society on 10 July 1926 as the stranger in *Oedipus at Colonus*. In 1927 Kit tragically contracted the disease Encephalitis lethargica, commonly known as 'sleeping sickness', and died in 1942 after a long illness. Richardson remarried on 26 January 1944. His new wife was Meriel ('Mu') Forbes, a member of the theatrical Forbes-Robertson family; their son Charles, known as 'Smallie', was born the following year. In 2002 the British Library purchased the papers and correspondence of Sir Ralph Richardson, including a large number of love letters and notes to his wife as 'Ferret' or 'Ferrety', a selection of which are shown here. They bear eloquent witness to the acting knight's deep attachment to his wife. 🐾

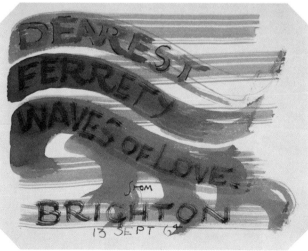

DEAREST
FERRETY
WAVES OF LOVE.
FROM
BRIGHTON
13 SEPT 64

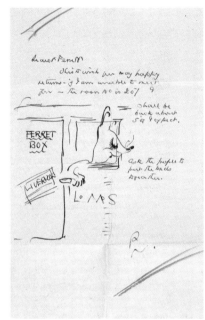

25 June 1969

The Prescription
Lady Richardson
Chester Terrace, NW1
To be taken with love.

RR (Doctor)

Undated
Dearest Ferret,
This is to wish you many happy
returns – if I am unable to meet you –
the room is no 207.
Shall be back about 5 o'clock I expect.
Ask the people to put the beds
together.
R.

X

Cambridge was our courtship.
Not the colleges, or such precincts,
But everything from the Mill bridge
Towards Grantchester. Those river meadows,
Three or four square miles contained it
Ornamented with willows, + green level,
Full drooping willows + sukes, + mallard + swans,
Or stumpy pollard willows + the dark silence
Of the slippery lapsing Cam. That was our place.
Not spoiled by precedent, for either of us.
We walked on neat macadam or dusty paths,
And sat on benches, + the skyline
All around was willows + cyclists — suspended,
In the watery weedy dream, the
An aquarium interval of slow
Waltzing figures, among glimpses
Of crumbling parapets, a horizon
Sinking below sea level. It was always dark.
One by one we made the public benches
Sacred to us. What did we talk about?
The University was a delay, a sentence
To be gone with + escaped.
Our only life was to come. Suspended
We hung there, magic or life, seeing
The scenery flow past like the silent river.
Were we actually going anywhere?
Were we exploring? Or talking away
Bewilderment, or trying word-shapes
To make hopes visible. We talked.
What a locked garden the world seemed then
When we walked past the gate, talking + talking.
We did not know what wings felt like.
Were what we felt wings?

'Cambridge was our courtship'

In late 2008, following the death of Ted Hughes, Poet Laureate and one of the most influential literary figures of the post-war generation, the British Library acquired all the papers remaining with his Estate. At the heart of this exceptional collection are the manuscripts relating to the volume *Birthday Letters*, Hughes's collection of poems that chart and explore his relationship with the poet Sylvia Plath, whom he met in February 1956 while both were studying in Cambridge. They married in June the same year and had two children, Frieda in 1960 and Nicholas in 1962, but by the time of Plath's suicide in 1963, she and Hughes had already separated. Hughes always remained resolutely silent on his life with Plath and her suicide, until 1995, when a small selection of the 'Birthday Letters' poems were unveiled in 'New Selected'. Then in 1998, Hughes published *Birthday Letters*, a series of eighty-eight powerful and intimate poems, written over a twenty-five-year period, about his troubled relationship with Plath and his reaction to her death. The poems are written in an open, tender, conversational language that addresses Plath directly. In this previously unpublished poem, Hughes reflects on their early courtship in Cambridge. *Birthday Letters* received widespread critical acclaim and a number of literary honours, including the T. S. Eliot prize for poetry and the Whitbread Book of the Year. 🍏

Cambridge was our courtship.
Not the colleges, or such precincts,
But everything from the Millbridge
Towards Grantchester. Those river meadows,
Three or four square miles contained it
Ornamented with willows, & green levels,
Full drooping willows & rushes, & mallard, & swans,
Or stumpy pollard willows & the dank silence
Of the slipping lapsing Cam. That was our place,

Not spoiled by precedent, for either of us.
We walked on neat macadam, on dusty paths,
And sat on benches & the skyline
All around was willows & cyclists – suspended,
In the watery, weedy, dream,
An aquarium interval of slow
Waltzing figures, among glimpses
Of crumbling parapets, a horizon
Sinking below sea level. It was always dark.
One by one we made the public benches
Sacred to us. What did we talk about?
The University was a delay, a sentence
To be borne with & escaped.
Our only life was to come. Suspended
We hung there moving our legs, seeing
The scenery flow past like the silent river,
Were we actually going anywhere?
Were we exploring? Or talking away
Bewilderment, or trying word-shapes
To make hopes visible. We talked.
What a locked garden the world seemed then,
When we walked past the gate, talking & talking.
We did not know what wings felt like.
Were what we felt wings?

Page 1: Detail of letter on page 2 (see below)

Page 2: Detail of letter by Mervyn Peake to his wife, Maeve Gilmore, 17 August 1950. Add Ms 88931/13/3/1/3

14, 17: British Library, Papyrus 42

15: © The British Museum

16: © The British Museum

18, 20–21: British Library, Add Ms 43490, f.23

19: British Library, Add Ms 35215, f.5

22: British Library, Egerton Ms 616, f.14

24: © Philip Mould Ltd/Bridgeman Art Library

25: © Philip Mould Ltd/Bridgeman Art Library

26: British Library, Stowe Ms 955, f.6

28: British Library, Stowe Ms 955, f.5v

29: British Library, Stowe Ms 955, f.17

30: British Library, Kings Ms 9, f.66v

32: British Library, Kings Ms 9, f.231v

33: (left) British Library, Stowe Ms 956, f.1v, (right) © Dean and Chapter of Ripon Cathedral

34: British Library, Lansdowne Ms 1236, f.9

36: National Portrait Gallery

37: British Library, Royal Ms 2A xvi, f.3

38: British Library, Add Ms 74286, ff.33v

40–41: British Library, Add Ms 74286, ff.33, 33v;

42: British Library, 688.l.13, opp.p.51

43: British Library, Egerton Ms 2572, f.11

44, 47: British Library, Harley Ms 4762, f.14

46: Mary Baskerville, later Mary Scudamore, by Marcus Gheeraerts the Younger (1615), © National Portrait Gallery, London

48, 51: British Library, Add Ms 42153, f.5

50: British Library, 10922.g.1, f.p

52, 56, 57: British Library, Harley Ms 6987, ff.157, 158

54: British Library, 193.a.1, f.p

55: British Library, 688.l.13, opp.p.67

58: British Library, Add Ms 33975, f.60v

59: British Library, 10906.dd.23, f.p

61: British Library, 688.l.13, opp.p.133

62, 66, 67: British Library, Add Ms 47608, ff.67, 68, 68v

64: Lady Mary Fenwick in mourning dress, holding a miniature of her husband, © Fitzwilliam Museum, Cambridge

65: British Library, 9503.h.1, p.102

68, 71: British Library, Add Ms 39839, f.42

69: British Library 10862.ee.34, pl.iv

70: British Library 010854.G.11, opp.p.178

72, 75: British Library, Egerton Ms 1614, ff.125v, 126

73: © National Maritime Museum

74: British Library, 10825.b.45, f.p

76, 80, 81: British Library, Add Ms 43689, ff.2, 3v

78: British Library, Dexter 316/126 (detail)

79: Private Collection/Bridgeman Art Library

82: British Library, Add Ms 38732D

84: (top) British Library, B.511876, p.22, (bottom) Brussels Brontë Society

85: British Library, Add Ms 38732C

86: British Library, Add Ms 43487, f.49

89: (left) British Library, 1162.h.2, f.p. and (right) 1203.g.3, opp.p.52

90: British Library, Add Ms 65530, f.9r

92: Wellcome Collection

93: British Library, Ashley 712

94: British Library, Add Ms 52332, f.52r

97: (left) Birmingham Museum and Art Gallery and (right) Metropolitan Museum of Art, New York

98: British Library, Ashley Ms 1376, f.16

99: British Library, 010920.f.20, f.p

100, 105: British Library, Add Ms 50141A, ff.1, 40v

104: British Library, c.131.f.11

106–111: British Library, Add Ms 88957/1/1

112, 114–115: British Library, Add Ms 83315, ff.52v, 51, 51v

116: © National Portrait Gallery, London, photo by Bassano

117: Private Collection/Ken Welsh/ Bridgeman Art Library

118: British Library, Add Ms 82391

121: British Library, 01087.l.4, p.358, f.p. (photographs) and Add Ms 82391 (envelope)

122: British Library, Add Ms 62892, f.150r

125: National Portrait Gallery, London

126–129: British Library, Add Ms 88918/13/3/1/1

131: British Library, Add Ms 89164/4/7, Gerry Raffles to Joan Littlewood 1/11/1948

133: Gerry Raffles and Joan Littlewood in New York, 1964, by Henry Grossman. British Library Add MS 89164/10/156

134, 136, 137: British Library, Ralph Richardson Archive, Add Ms 82066-67

138: British Library, Add Ms 88918

140: Mortimer Rare Book Room, Smith College, USA, and the Estate of Ted Hughes

Andrea Clarke is Lead Curator of Medieval and Early Modern Manuscripts at the British Library. She co-curated the Library exhibitions 'Henry VIII: Man and Monarch' with David Starkey in 2009 and 'Leonardo da Vinci: A Mind in Motion' in 2019. She is author of *Tudor Monarchs: Lives in Letters* (British Library, 2017).

First published in 2011

This edition first published in 2020 by
The British Library
96 Euston Road
London NW1 2DB

Text copyright © Andrea Clarke, 2011, 2020

Illustrations copyright © The British Library, 2011, 2020, and other named copyright holders (see pages 142–3)

The British Library would like to thank the following for their kind permission to reproduce letters in this book: Merlin Holland (Oscar Wilde, *De Profundis*), Professor Jon Stallworthy (Rupert Brooke to Cathleen Nesbitt), Josa Young (Roger Keyes to his wife Eva), The Estate of Mervyn Peake (Mervyn Peake to his wife Maeve Gilmore), Peter Rankin (Gerry Raffles to Joan Littlewood), The Trustees of The Ralph and Meriel Richardson Foundation (Ralph Richardson to his wife Meriel Forbes), The Estate of Ted Hughes (Ted Hughes).

Cataloguing in Publication Data
A catalogue record for this publication is available from the British Library

ISBN 978 0 7123 5351 9

Design and typesetting by
Andrew Barron and Georgie Hewitt

Printed and bound in the Czech Republic by PB Tisk